YOUR CAREER
GAME

YOUR CAREER GAME

Hap Vaughan

John Wiley & Sons

New York   Chichester   Brisbane   Toronto   Singapore

Reproduction or translation of any part of this work
beyond that permitted by Section 107 or 108 of the
1976 United States Copyright Act without the permission
of the copyright owner is unlawful. Requests for
permission or further information should be addressed to
the Permissions Department, John Wiley & Sons, Inc.

This publication is designed to provide accurate and
authoritative information in regard to the subject
matter covered. It is sold with the understanding that
the publisher is not engaged in rendering legal, accounting,
or other professional service. If legal advice or other
expert assistance is required, the services of a competent
professional person should be sought. *From a Declaration
of Principles jointly adopted by a Committee of the
American Bar Association and a Committee of Publishers.*

Library of Congress Cataloging in Publication Data

Vaughan, Hap.
    Your career game.

    Bibliography: p.
    Includes Index.
    1. Career development.   I. Title.
HF5549.5.C35V38 1987   650.1'4   87-20964
ISBN 0-471-62948-0
ISBN 0-471-62949-9 (Paperback)

Printed in the United States of America

10 9 8 7 6 5 4 3 2 1

Preface

This book is a response to the reactions of audiences to a series of discussions I began conducting several years ago on the subject of career management. While the discussion presents at least six themes, it boils down to two main ones: You have personal potential greater than anything you have yet dreamed, and every person creates his or her own success or failure in a company.

Repeatedly, audiences have told me they have thought about some of the concepts I describe, but they have never before brought all the concepts together to form a *system* that they could *use*. This is what I have shown them how to do and what this book aims to show you. This book is my effort to convince you of how simple the process of career management is, and how great the rewards are.

My differences from many of the "experts" in career management are clearcut. My message is *how to use your company* to create shared success that both you and your company need. *Their* message, most often, is simply how to find another job in another company. I define success in your career as a balance between doing satisfying work *and* earning the pay you need. Your pay and increases are more important than many managers or academics know or admit.

This is a success book and not a "win" book, except in the sense of playing a game with yourself. I urge you to define and achieve the career *you* want, to use yourself effectively in your company, and to get your share of your company's success. Nothing in my presentation encourages the popular theme of the success sellers, "You can be whatever you want." I do not address that issue. Rather, I am convinced and want to convince you that merely adding a little management to your career will greatly increase your share of success in your company.

Your problem is not how to write a snappy résumé, how to look out for number one, how to beat out peer competition, how to move to a new company, or inadequate education. Similarly, it is not to search inside yourself and find the one great ultimate assignment for which you are destined. Something attracted you to your present company. It could have been a default, a port in a storm. No matter. What matters is using your present company and your present people to begin achieving success.

I have invited challenges to my approach, and I have received them. Academics and high-level managers say I emphasize pay too much. They say it reflects kinks in my value system or tends to stir up unrealistic expectations. Interestingly, both sources applaud my ideas of the essential relationship between companies and people. Another common challenge comes from skeptics in management and the ranks alike who say, "You can't do it that way in *my* company."

Regarding pay, the managers' advice, "Work hard and trust us," contradicts even elementary ideas of measurable goals. It does not allow you the personal control you need. The taint that academics assign to money is equally unrealistic to me. Pay goals are a good device for assigning value to work goals.

I have not heard "You can't do it that way" from anyone who has tried. I have not met anyone who has committed and set goals who did not achieve them or an achievement of equal value.

There is a fortunate balance between the needs of our society for work and the innate personal satisfaction we get from doing our work. That balance is the foundation on which you can build a satisfying career and company association.

Do not be confused by the career guides that give you the impression that you're searching for the one great zenith of work, the job that is your ultimate travail in which you are meant to shine. It just isn't so! These are misconceptions fostered by people who never learned the game. The exact opposite is true. There are hundreds of jobs that you never thought of that will satisfy you or move you through your career. You can find satisfaction in them, changing them to be even more satisfying and productive, and you will move on and up to do it again, if you let yourself. In each job, you will wonder how there can be such a succession of challenges.

HAP VAUGHAN

Dallas, Texas
September 1987

Contents

SECTION TWO
The Money Game

SECTION THREE
Doing It!

The Career Game

1

Personal Success Patterns

Using success patterns to achieve personal success is a skill you can learn. By learning how your *company* works, you can design ways of using your company to create personal success. By changing the way *you* work, you can be on the path toward getting your share of your company's success, thus making the company the tool of your personal success.

Your first successes will be simple ones, achieved by your deliberate plans. Though small, these first successes will open entirely new visions of and expectations for a larger personal share of your company's successes. No later or greater successes will be more important to you than those first ones that confirm that you can create success for yourself in your company. Those will be eye-openers to your immense personal potential; they will confirm that you can succeed by using your plans to achieve your goals.

SUCCESS

We all have bits and pieces of a definition of "success." We recognize the conflicts and competition among success in our family, social, and career activities. I believe that success is achieving personal goals. Those goals may be vague, but they exist. I want to pin down a definition of success useful for our discussions. Although this definition is a simple one, it was not simple to create.

Career success is two things:

> Doing work that satisfies you

> Earning the pay you need

The first is easy to agree upon. But many people are reluctant to admit to themselves, and particularly to someone else, that earning good pay is a career goal of nearly equal importance to doing satisfying work. At home, in school, and at work, money and pay may be downgraded as primary measures of career success:

> Keep your nose to the grindstone and your eye to the goal designed for you. Surely, as the sun rises in the East, the value of your work will be recognized and The Company will assign you more valuable tasks—and give you more pay.

That's baloney! But that's the dream embedded in many minds.

Top executives are the ones who least practice such a philosophy. They know that pay is a true indicator of their value to their company. It compensates their families for the price they pay, and it looks great when published. But, for us there is no better expression of the value our company assigns to our work than the pay it gives us. Congratulate me. Compliment me. Pat me on the back. But give me money! Each check confirms that my work is valuable. Each raise tells me that the company thinks I continue to grow.

In your gut, you may know this but may not consciously face it. You may go home from work and get a twist inside. You may refuse to recognize that the work you've grown used to is no longer valuable enough to earn you the pay you need.

I don't mean to assign excessive weight to pay as a measure of career success. However, I believe that it is as important as satisfying work, but not more so. What is more important is that you fully evaluate your own feelings as you define what career success is for you. You must understand that it is a part of the foundation for your career management.

Career success is only a part of life success. To be worthwhile, to satisfy you, you must create a balance between your career success and your other life achievements.

COMPANY

To use your company effectively to achieve your personal goals, you must have an understanding of what any company is—*a continuing association of a group of people working together to achieve shared goals.*

This definition applies to a church, a school, a Boy Scout troop. But it is vital to your view of the business company in which you work.

It will take a long time to automatically think of "My" company, or "Our" company, rather than "The" company. I don't propose that this become a fetish. "The" company is a concept so deeply embedded in society that many will never purge it. But building the "My" company feeling into personal career goals is a positive boost.

The Company: "They"

Along with thinking and speaking about "The" company, we also think and speak of "They." "They" are people and activities *in* our company but *apart* from us. We assign "Them" the responsibility for the mistakes our company makes. But we also assign "Them" the responsibility and credit for our success.

There is no "They" in our company; "They" don't exist. *We* do the work. *We* create the success of our company.

SOURCE OF SUCCESS

You and I are the vitality of our companies, the force and power behind our growth and profitability. But few of us are aware of the personal excellence that makes our companies successful.

We imagine a gap in our companies' organization: We see ourselves in our work groups and picture our executive managers as separate and remote, with a gap in between filled with successful people who are more excellent than *we are*. There is no such gap! There are no such people! There are no people more excellent than we are. We perform the excellent work and management that make our companies successful.

This is a vital theme which you need for your personal success: *Your work and your management are superb. You must realize that your own excellence is the source of your company's excellence.*

Personally accepting this theme has a direct relationship to changing your career approach. If you can contribute even a small amount to managing and operating your company, you can use similar techniques to manage your own career.

Surely you have observed that peoples' capabilities and contributions vary widely. The reasons are many: differences in intelligence, energy, personal manner, goal identification, supervision, and so on. In the same sense, people work differently; some work best in emergencies, others work best in routine situations. Regardless of these differences, you must realize that a small, self-controlled, sustained improvement will increase your value to your company.

PERSONAL VALUE

It is important to understand your personal value and potential. For the moment, keep these two points in mind: First, you are a contributor to and sharer of the success of your company. Second, your present contribution is good compared with others', but low compared with your potential. In other words, a moderate change—growth—in your contribution will lead to a significant increase of your share of success.

I am speaking of a *change* in your contribution, rather than an increase in your contribution, that is, a change in how you use yourself rather than an increase in either the time or effort that you apply to your work. As your success grows, you may decide to work harder or longer, but that is not a part of the present discussion. The point is: *better* use of self, not *more* use of self.

THE PATTERNS

I began realizing early in my career that there are patterns associated with personal success. The first patterns of success I recognized were important, but they were small and disconnected. I have an early memory of using my company's open-door policy for a frank personal discussion with my boss, two levels up. I badly needed more pay. I had sense enough to know that my problem was how to increase my value to the company so that my boss could increase my pay. He was surprised but receptive. Our talk was helpful to both of us, to our later relationship, and to my pay. I made this a personal pattern, and used it sparingly but effectively.

A short time afterward, I began to use the tactic which I will discuss later as "underground projects." I became aware that other people were using success patterns, in most cases unknowingly.

A little over five years later I was privileged to participate in the planning of an exciting company that grew almost explosively. I was amazed at the results produced by effective planning and control. The miracle of goal setting and goal seeking became a reality. I was astounded by the audacious goals developed and how regularly we succeeded. I could hardly believe the major achievements that we were deliberately making happen.

Then I realized that the same success system used by my company was largely applicable to my own career. I'm not sure that I recognized at first how closely the success patterns of a company and the people that make up the company are bound together, but two things soon became clear to me: First, the system I needed for my career was basically a modification of the system that my company used. (Later, I realized that this is nothing less than the system used for all management.) Second, and inseparable from those flashes of insight, I developed a fairly radical personal goal: to divert from my engineering background and become the controller of my division, in a little less than three years.

Did it work? Like a miracle! Better than I could have imagined. I was promoted to controller in two years, so far ahead of my plan that I hadn't finished my basic course in accounting. When it happened, it happened fast. But the time and personal learning was an expensive process for me. Learning the simple system by which to define my goals and control my career took me ten years. But the real learning, the insights and understanding of it all, came in only the last few months of that time. If I had not worked in two superb companies, it could have taken twice that long, or it may have never happened.

I know that many intelligent people spend their whole careers without ever understanding the game, the career management system. But I also know that what took me ten years to learn can be learned in only a few hours.

TACTICS

There are minor patterns of career success that I call tactics. You can develop them for yourself, and you can adapt the tactics of other people. You can use similar tactics, with modifications, to succeed repeatedly. You can also use a simple basic management system for your personal career management: develop your job goal, make your plan—milestones, schedule, tactics, resources, and so forth—then control your progress as you execute your plan.

This is a forgiving system, a soft system. You can use all or any of its parts to produce the success you want. Used alone, tactics can lead you to incredible achievements. But even a simple, systematic approach will work miracles for you in improved job opportunities and pay. Using either approach is a change—not additional work—to how you presently manage your career.

Career tactics are personal success patterns deliberately used to produce success in recurrent work situations. When you recognize an opportunity or problem, you adapt and use a tactic that has been successful for you before in that kind of situation.

Your tactics often originate when a spontaneous action doesn't work well, or even fails to solve a problem. You say, "The next time this happens, I'm going to do 'so and so,'" and you design a tactic to use the next time that kind of situation arises. It is a solution waiting for a problem that you expect to recur.

Tactics are not vague ideas or general approaches. They are similar even among different people. Tactics may be used recurrently. Some are so recurrent that I give them names. When I use these names in discussion groups, I see smiles of recognition by people who have never heard of them before. Those who smile are always right when they explain what "October triumph" and "underground projects" are; only my names are new; they've had the problems before.

Consider a job performance review as an opportunity for a good, continuing tactical plan. Even in companies that have good systems of personal performance review, few employees use them as part of their planned career advancement. Most people approach their review as a burden instead of an opportunity. Often supervisors who support the purpose of the system flinch at the administrative burden required to make it work.

But stand back, supervisor! I will do most of the work for my own performance review. I will design my job—and my pay—to meet both our needs, and I will help to create our expectations for next year.

In developing such a plan, it is important to evaluate both your goals and the correct approach to your supervisor. Consider the people and goals of your work group. You may want to go for the impossible but not the absolutely impossible. Consider what you can and can't do. For instance, if your pay increase is lower than you expected, you probably can't get it raised in the interview. But you can begin to lay the groundwork for a better raise next time. This is the first of several actions you will take before your next review to influence the raise you will get then. Of course, these pay expectations must be consistent with the expected growth of the value of your work.

Even the seemingly impossible may be possible. Consider this actual case of someone who went to a performance review prepared for the worst. Trev knew he had earned a bonus. But times were bad and he suspected his boss was weak. Weak works both ways, though. Trev had had a very successful project, but unfortunately it was completed early in the year. Both Trev and his supervisor had been congratulated by a memo at the time. Trev didn't receive a bonus. He was disappointed but immediately put Plan B into action. Holding eye contact with Mr. Weak, he discussed the fairness of the situation, reminding him of the source and content of their congratulations from upper management. Firmly, but with control, Trev said that he felt he was being dealt with unfairly. The result? Several weeks later he received his bonus.

That's a true but unusual case. It illustrates that the situation wouldn't have been corrected unless Trev had gone prepared to try to correct it. An effective plan for performance review requires preparation. Build a brief folder of notes from before and after the review. Concentrate on defining the assignments and job opportunities that you want. Spend 50 to 80 percent of your part of the discussion on these matters. Your future and your growth depend on expanding your work assignments in the period until your next review.

Ask for assignments where you'll need your supervisor's help or attention. You don't have to stress that point, but take the initiative to get your supervisor involved in your career. Discuss the plan you offered for yourself in your last review, even if your review wasn't with that supervisor. If your overall performance has been good, you can soft-pedal the problems, but be prepared to discuss them.

Finally, don't save problems for discussion in your review. Solve problems as part of your everyday work. Keep an open line with your supervisor because you need it. Then the performance review becomes a review of shared successes.

Will It Work?

How much can you influence your own review? Beyond anything that you have imagined! Here's an actual case. I discussed this tactic with a skeptical young man, explained how he could both write the script for his performance review and assure himself of an unusually large pay raise.

He started early. His twin approaches were to define his personal goals and his plan, and to express them in the context of the company's procedures. He read the procedures on performance review, learning their structure and terminology. He made early, low-keyed comments to his supervisor about his work goals and plans, and his pay ambitions. Later, he gave his supervisor a brief summary of his job plan. He scheduled all of this and his other activities consistently with the company's schedule of performance review.

After his review, he could hardly wait to tell me how well his plan had worked! His supervisor had fed back to him nearly all of his own self-evaluation and work plans. His raise was even more than he expected.

That is what is supposed to happen. The young man had developed an excellent plan to increase his work contribution, within the needs of his work group, for the next year. His supervisor concurred, with minor changes and suggestions. Increasing his pay was confirmation of commitments achieved, shared expectations of his plans for the next year, and a new commitment of his company to give him a greater share of its success. He, in turn, had set his own goals against which he and his supervisor would measure his performance in the next year.

IS IT TOO LATE?

All of this sounds great if you're five or ten years into your career. But what good can a personal success plan do for you if you're at age forty-five plus?

I work with people in their mid-forties who are reworking their careers. One man, now over fifty and going strong, made a late start—passed up college, saw the light, got his degree, and started fulfilling his ambition late. When I met him at forty-two, he was beginning to make changes in the way he worked, in how he used himself. He said the idea that I called "success patterns" had been dawning on him for several years.

This man's interest and motivation were stirred by realizations that his career had definitely topped out. While this was obvious in his pay raises, he was more concerned that the challenging, interesting assignments were going to younger people. Realistically, he knew that his company's expectations for him had settled into the "good ol' boy" category. His situation was intolerable to him; he was preparing for action.

He was excited to discuss the concept of a whole system of success. It was his kind of game, and he played it as that—not a trivial pursuit, but an exciting risk play. I was surprised by the cleverness of his plays and the concentrations he included in them for the needs of others.

Early in our association I saw major changes in this person's tactics. They reflected his new realization that the company (particularly the people senior to him) *needed* his success, his ideas, and his willingness to make changes and champion innovations. He learned that these senior people want to be used, to be a part of his plans. His new contacts offered his own people a new entry to other levels and areas of the company.

I have watched this man's game for more than ten years now. His string of successes is a string of miracles, as much to him as to me. He continues to play it as a game. He makes big commitments and takes the associated risks, but he succeeds. This fellow started late—twice. He is fortunate in having much to offer, but probably not more than millions of people who never realize the career game they're playing.

AGGRESSIVE?

After several years of discussing these concepts of success patterns with groups, a participant once prefaced a question to me with, "When I change to this aggressive approach to career management . . . ." For the first time I became aware that I had never recommended an aggressive career approach; nor have I ever recommended against one.

I recommend a *deliberate* approach: Think your actions through well before you move. This approach requires commitment: You must dedicate small portions of your personal time to make it work. You must practice personal control: When you miss a planned achievement or a schedule, you must take action to get back on the track. But personal aggressiveness is not an essential element of career success at the levels I am discussing.

How about competition? Will you encounter competitive situations? Yes, probably a few. You may be contending with others for the same assignments or jobs. In these situations, organize and pursue a solid, well-considered approach. Your chance of succeeding will be high. However, if you fail, you will probably be offered another equally attractive opportunity within the next six weeks.

Also remember that below executive job levels, in nearly any good company with moderate growth, there is almost no competition.

PERSONAL GROWTH AND RENEWAL

Continuing to develop those personal attributes that initially made you valuable is essential to continuing your good relationship with your company, and to your self-respect.

Knowledge is among the most volatile of personal resources. Estimates are that half of the value of a college education becomes obsolete in five to ten years. But don't jump to the conclusion that returning to school is your solution. It may well be a good thing to do, but your continual personal growth and renewal may be first served by your work. All work now has an accelerating rate of obsolescence; if you don't become an agent of change in your work, be assured that some competitor will.

There are many resources for personal development in the work itself. They start with the people in your work group; observe, acquire, adapt, and extend the best that they have. Expand your horizons to nearby areas and do the same. Read in your field and associated fields. Join with outsiders in similar and associated work. After that, consider continuing your education in school.

Must you use resources in this sequence? Certainly not. It's excellent to decide early that you will return to school. Just don't forget that your best opportunity for continuing personal development is your work itself.

Failing to grow and to renew your personal value will deny you the major elements of career success: You will share fewer satisfying work assignments and your share of pay will fall below your expectations and needs. But most of all, you will have a reduced sense of satisfaction in your work.

STARTING OUT

I can cite many examples illustrating how to start, but they may not apply to everyone's situation and personal style. One thing is the same for everyone, however: You start by deciding to *do it*; you *commit* to execute your career on *your* plan. You may need to change your plan to take advantage of new opportunities that you discover or that are offered by your company. You may change because you decide your plans are wrong, or something else is more attractive.

Making the decision to change is your start of real change. Someone or something may trigger that decision. It may be my words or others', a change in your company, or a change in your personal situation, to make you decide and commit to change. Their decision for action is a combination of "I can" and "I will." The "I can" part comes from realizing the patterns of your own successes and the success patterns of others, some far less endowed.

Once you decide to change, I urge you to schedule six weeks in which to set your goals. The schedule is an essential part of the decision. However, some people work on a slower schedule. Recently I spoke with a woman who had made a major step up. She grinned and said, "Well, you made me do it." She said that she had made her decision more than a year before when we had talked. She had been in her assignment over fifteen years. She was an excellent, widely respected contributor, but her position was far below her potential. She is a quiet, shy person and when we had talked earlier, I thought that she would never decide to manage herself—but she did.

She waited and watched for openings. Her qualifications made her successful in getting her opening, but she was also lucky. She waited and watched for her opportunity. But that's a dangerous game—the job may have been given to someone else. So shy or not, I suggest you use feelers and probes to spot opportunities before they become generally visible. Many of the best openings are filled before they become known.

There's another aspect to getting a new assignment. When you lay the groundwork to ask for another assignment, be prepared to identify and suggest your replacement. Suggest someone with competence; you may return to the job above that person. You should also realize that the person leaving the job you want may also be suggesting his or her replacement, and it may not be you. Does that give you even more ideas?

In another case, I hadn't talked with one particular man for well over a year. He invited me to speak to a class that he was teaching. I had forgotten him, a mistake of mine, because I had assumed that he would never make the decision to change the slow-paced path he was following. He was a schoolteacher and intended to stay in teaching. Unknown to me, he had committed himself to change when I first talked to the faculty at his school. He decided to discuss his own plans with his supervisor. He reviewed his goals and his supporting plans, which he had only recently solidified. His supervisor was receptive and agreeable but had shown surprise at the intensity of the young man's desire for advancement.

That is a common problem. Often, people who are quiet and appear satisfied with their present achievements are assumed to have limited ambitions. How do you solve that problem? By assuring yourself that your supervisor understands your desire and your need for personal growth. This is not a situation for inference and indirect reference. Even if you're shy, or if your supervisor is shy, *you* must assure that there's a clear understanding between you—what specific work you want, and what your pay expectations are.

In my later conversation with this young man, he spoke of the quiet revolution he had made in his life, particularly in his financial situation. He reaffirmed my advice of giving balanced attention to pay goals. Just prior to our second conversation, he had bought both a house and a new car. He said that in the early stages of shaping his plans, he realized that even improving his rate of advancement in his primary job wouldn't satisfy the needs for income that he had set for himself, money that he felt he now needed for family and self. His solution was to teach evening classes in a local junior college. His subject? Career management. When I met with his class, I could feel that they had caught his expectations toward career management.

YOUR WAY

There is no prefab solution to *your* opportunity, *your* problem. Neither I nor anyone can offer one with honesty, but you will not have a problem if you can get past step one: commitment and goal setting. If you commit and set goals, you will find a way.

Everyone I have worked with who has set goals has succeeded— no exceptions. This does not include those people who "try it out." I don't depreciate the tryouts; a few tryouts evolve into commitments. But commitment is the real turning point. Those who commit solve their problems.

After you commit, I recommend the cold-turkey approach. Set your personal goals in six weeks. I see that work often and best, but I see the slow approach work sometimes.

In Chapter 14, I will discuss the general management system—the classic three-step method of managing goal seeking. It will give you a specific framework for career management.

THE CHANGE

For many people this approach to personal management is a major change. They have always been willing to work, to be used by their company. They are used to starting a day or a year with an attitude frequently expressed as "I will do the best I can. I will meet the problems and opportunities as they come. I will solve and use them as best I can." But that attitude won't get you what you need—or what your company needs.

Deliberate goal seeking is a completely different game. You look ahead and *commit* that by next month, on the 31st, you will have accomplished something specific, something of value, maybe something you need, maybe something you don't presently know how to accomplish. Your "something" is a stretch, an expansion of your person. It is a segment of career growth—more satisfying work, a step to more pay.

TENSION?

What about tension? You have it now; you may still have it. But you may gain control of your tension if the word "deliberate" acquires more significance for you. Setting goals which you have high expectations of achieving may help. Start now to expect a few failures, a few tears, real or imaginary. Back off from a few goals; you'll have another go at them later, but intend to have enough failures to measure the increase in your capability. If your company or your supervisor won't tolerate any failures, conceal them by lowering the level of your goals that you expose.

Don't aim to conquer the world tomorrow. Don't worry that you don't know how to achieve something now; you will find a way. Put a little risk in your early goals, but balance it with a high probability of success.

Try a simple means for testing and experimenting. For example, if you are a clerk with an idea to shrink the files by 50 percent, try it on the sly. Put a small code on the file items you intend to remove or destroy. Then put an activity mark (month and year) on any of those items that you use. If you feel gamey, pull and hide some bulky, inactive part of the file. That way you're covered. There's no better way of proving that it's dispensable; just don't go on vacation without restoring the file. Take the initiative with these experiments. Then make the proposal to your supervisor.

If you're a supervisor you have more chances to experiment, and more chances for success, than in any other capacity. Use ideas from the many popular books that exist—some have interesting gimmicks—or try old faithful approaches, or think of your own approach. You can almost bet that any continued recognition of good performance is going to be successful because there isn't enough of it. Go easy at first; you may shock somebody. Try brief performance discussions with your people every two months or more often. Use variety in your comments to them. Make a few notes before or after your talks.

If you're a planner, take the initiative and design the plan for a project. Spot an upcoming requirement and sketch an approach for handling it. Think through the reception you expect when you propose it, and adapt the plan accordingly. If you think an innovative approach will work, go after one. Otherwise, stick with a well-considered, plain-vanilla proposal.

What's common in these suggestions? *Doing it yourself. Taking the initiative.* Risk may also be common, but you can control your exposure to risk by anticipating it, by your personal style, by avoiding encroachment, and by how and to whom you talk.

A DON'T DO

Many people approach me because they feel stalled in their careers. Most of them realize that the responsibility and initiative belong to them. Almost always, their common impulse is to look for a job in another company. I tell them not to do it. That impulse is wrong. Another company or another supervisor may be needed, but the problem is more likely fundamental and personal.

When economic times are good, the air is electrified with invitations to change companies. The classified ads, books on résumé writing, letters, even long-distance phone calls all suggest, "Change companies." That may be good advice for some, but for most it means throwing away a major part of the personal investment in a career. Or worse, it may mean losing an opportunity now to recognize and correct a career problem that will continue in any company.

Before you make the possible mistake of moving, consider whether the same effort required to make a move might earn you a far bigger return if you invested it in your present company. Consider whether your real problem is *how you are using your present company*.

Also, if you are considering a change, you can afford a little more risk in career experimentation in your present company. Consider it; you may never have such a good opportunity to try things, to test whether you can make the system work for you, to succeed at the game.

In most cases, changing companies is a temporary stimulus at best, a patch that wears off without solving a deeper problem. To really manage your career, you must learn to take care of yourself in your company, to use the company. Don't decide to leave without mature consideration of the value of your present company associations.

I said previously that a company is a "continuing association of people . . . . ." That definition was urged on me by a young audience after a discussion of a career strategy I call "company hopping." I believe nearly all of them accepted my theme that each of us has a strong personal need to sustain the bonds that develop between us and a good company.

If you decide to change companies after you have given full weight to these factors, *go for it*.

EXCELLENCE IN PRESENT WORK

Managing your career is as important to you, and to your company, as performing the primary tasks of your present job. But your first priority is to perform well in the tasks of your current assignment.

There is no conflict in these two priorities. Make career management an integral part of your everyday work. Much of it involves thought processes that are natural parts of the routine of a job. You will do much of your managing and planning away from the job; some of your best ideas may come in the morning hours before work, and on the way home from work.

How much time does the full career-managing system require? About the equivalent of 2 percent of the time you spend at work. Only a small part of this time will come from your work schedule. It's great stuff to muse about in the shower or when you're cutting the grass.

Keep it light; make it fun; make it your goal-seeking game. Don't let it become a big thing. Most of all, don't let it reduce the excellence of your present work, for that is the foundation of your future successes.

2

How Good Am I?

You are three to ten times as good as you presently think you are.

If you don't recognize your excellence—and use it—you can spend a lifetime without fulfilling your potential. Gifted people are rare and the waste of gifted people is tragic. But that waste is nothing compared with the massive waste of the extraordinary capabilities of large numbers of ordinary people.

Over and over, I see people come to realize that they are fundamentally much better than their present performance. They begin experimenting, playing the game. They always succeed. Time after time they say, "I can't believe I didn't try this before."

The responsibility for this waste of capability is largely our own. At worst, it can fall on our company only for a short time. We are responsible for ourselves.

Why do most of us use our extraordinary abilities so poorly? Because we never realize what tremendous potential ordinary people possess. Of the few who come to realize that power, or sense it innately, nearly all are baffled by how to put it to use, to exploit the potential, to fulfill the success that that potential is meant to support.

Our need for a means of fulfilling our potential is born only when we become aware of having the potential. Before that we have an excuse. But once that excuse is taken away, it's impossible to deny that great potential.

There's a bit of poetry that says it beautifully, an excerpt from Gray's *Elegy in a Country Churchyard*:

> *Full many a gem of purest ray serene*
> *The dark unfathomed caves of oceans bear:*
> *Full many a flower is born to blush unseen,*
> *To waste its sweetness on the desert air.*

You are a gem whose value I know better than you do. But you are not valued only for beauty, bound unmoving, dependent on others to fulfill your value. You are different. Within you there is a capability, an urge to move yourself to a realization of your destiny. Otherwise why are you reading this? You were not born to waste your ability in a self-created career desert.

I know that each of you has the personal ability to achieve the personal success that is essential to the success of your company. I haven't always known this. Like most, I evaluated people, and myself, in terms of what they are or do presently, not realizing what they could be or do. But as I grew in my company, I recognized the miracles of people blossoming around me. For example, I saw a young girl just out of high school move from incompetence—which I interpreted as dumbness—to real excellence in administrative work.

Years later, I worked with another young woman in whom I thought I saw the same pattern. When months passed without her blossoming, I was about ready to give up, to admit to myself that I was wrong. Then, there was a breakthrough. She came to me to discuss a problem she had solved. She analyzed it clearly. She explained the procedure she proposed for correcting it. That woman is on her way!

Again and again I have seen people of ordinary abilities inspired to make miracles in creating and making products, although it's true that I heard gripes and complaints on the way toward high goals and tough achievements.

Those were not the "good ol' days." Those days are today and tomorrow; I am still seeing the miracles. Some come as the dawning of a slow light. Others are flashes of great insights and energy. Their sources are people of all backgrounds, conditions, and ages.

Are you skeptical? Are you thinking, "If I'm as good as he says, why haven't I realized it before?" You haven't realized it because you, like most of us, are measuring yourself against an unrealistic standard. You have been conditioned by others, as well as by yourself, to use a standard that is not excellence, but perfection — the ultimate.

One indication of this unrealistic standard is the increasing use of the word "eclectic," the combination of the best of all things. Compared with an eclectic standard, all of our work — individual and company — is poorly performed. With some people, it's always popular to deplore our status; after all, compared with what it could be, it has to be poor. Worse, they compare our progress to these perfect standards.

These attitudes create the dilemma. On one hand, we feel that we are making excellent progress; on the other, we are told that our performance is poor. We resolve this dilemma by assuming that our performance is poor and that others must be doing the work that produces excellence. Who's doing all this excellent work? "Them", those mythical people in the "gap" which I mentioned in Chapter 1. "Somebody"—a bunch of people—have to be doing good because there's a lot of good being done! There must be a broad base to produce the excellence in our company. It's us; WE are excellent; WE produce the excellence in our company.

We have grown up with these assumptions that prevent us from recognizing our own potential. They're like masks put on us by someone else or created by ourselves. They either keep us from seeing reality or they distort our understanding. One assumption is based on origin:

> I come from a humble origin; don't expect great things of me; I am destined for a humble future. So I never consider setting high goals, stretching. My good judgment is confirmed; my modest achievements approximate those of my origins.

Another assumption is based on our history of grades in school. We let them become expectations: "I am poor in math; I will continue to be poor in math, even through college. Now I can expect a mediocre career."

This last assumption is particularly dangerous because there is some truth in it; until you demonstrate some work performance that is better than your grades, your grades are the best available measure of your performance. That barrier, if you have it, is one of the easiest to break.

People senior to us can also mask our ability so that we can't see it. They can insert images of incompetence into our minds. Recently I listened to a mechanic call his helper "dummy." He made scathing remarks about the helper's stupidity. The helper wasn't stupid, he was ignorant—he had the ability to learn but had not yet learned the skills he needed. The mechanic had failed him by not teaching him those skills. At times all of us are incompetent and ignorant; we need to understand that.

INCOMPETENCE

When people are first hired, neither they nor their supervisors should expect effective performance immediately. The new employee's need to learn and perform is a challenge, both for you and your supervisor. The supervisor should not regard a new employee as incompetent, but should expect the employee to become competent in six to nine months.

In lower-level jobs, of limited scope, we expect people to develop the whole breadth of skills associated with their work. However, with increasingly higher-level jobs the scope of knowledge and skills required may extend well beyond what one person can handle, and thus calls for a team. The teamwork necessary to cover the requirements of some jobs presents a set of new challenges and sources of satisfaction. It also presents a new set of realities: One person can no longer cover the whole, one person can no longer be competent in everything; we have moved beyond the renaissance person.

This need for help from others may give rise to self-doubts. While we may regard the chief's use of a consultant to handle a problem in higher math as an effective and natural action, when we need similar help, we feel it's a weakness. It's not. It is a reasonable incompetence as long as we recognize it and act to get our work done. Besides, each time we seek help, we learn a little more. Each time, we and those we consult exchange knowledge. These exchanges are common as we scale the ladder, both managerial and technical. There are good accountants and controllers who aren't good bookkeepers, and engineers who are poor drafters, and vice versa.

What is important is that the combination of skills and energy in the company and its work groups be effective, and that there be effective backups. As individuals move and advance, the realignments of work provide the opportunities needed for personal growth. The movement of people in and out of work groups is compensated by balancing the work requirements with combinations of people and their skill strengths.

A similar strategy of using complementary strengths can be used on a personal basis. For example, Jim had worked his way into a technical administrative job with minimal technical background. He had an intuitive understanding of the goal-seeking game and, with it, a clear understanding of his limitations and problems. He knew that, to succeed, he needed to compensate for his weakness in technical fields. On any assignment he seemed to identify the areas where he needed help. He was energetic and liked by many people. He organized his problems according to which consultants could best help. Often he got his information at lunch or coffee time. He didn't advertise his weakness, but he was unpretentious and frank. His consultants seemed to get real satisfaction from contributing to his success and growth. Jim acquired a lot of their knowledge; while he did not grow to be a technical giant, he developed an excellent portfolio of personal technical skills. His was a deliberately and carefully managed "incompetence."

MEASURING

Can you really measure how good you are, how much you are worth to your company? Not precisely. But a simple, two-question test will give you a good idea of the answer. The first question is the most important:

Do You Do What You Say You Will Do?

Nobody can answer yes unequivocally. If your answer is yes 80 to 90 percent of the time, you're close to perfect. Obviously, if you don't commit to do anything, your answer would be 100 percent of the time, but that's cheating.

The question should be answered for a period of six months to a year. Completing 90 percent of your commitments is great. If you do 100 percent, you're probably not taking on enough tough tasks; your commitments are short on challenge. That leads to the second question of the test:

Are You Continuing to Grow?

If you're commiting to and doing things that represent continuing personal growth, you must be good for your company. The company assigned you to your job because it thought you had the necessary qualifications. You achieve your part of the company's shared challenges, and the company shares your expectations of increased contributions from your continuing growth.

Don't expect to live up to your whole potential, but decide to do something—something that uses your potential. Ask yourself what you are going to do and set a timetable for doing it. You will do it, or most of it, by the time you set.

When you have decided that you will do something, make a few reserved commitments to your supervisor. Make committing to perform specific tasks part of your style, not just with your supervisor, but with the other people with whom you work. But first, make the commitment to yourself that you will do what you say you will do.

OVER-COMMITMENT

When you start on any path, you are almost sure to make commitments you can't keep. All of us start that way – underestimating the tasks. Correcting this seems to be a part of maturing. But don't correct it solely by setting longer schedules; put a little pressure on finding ways to shorten your performance schedules instead.

I was once assigned a great opportunity to manage a large manufacturing project. There were a half-dozen others in our group with about the same amount of experience – or inexperience. Several of us were eager to try new things. Each had at least one innovation in mind. We got into trouble, but it was great trouble! We found it was tough to get the routine work done and still have time for the innovations. We had to drop a few of the new things, but we achieved a large proportion of the improvements to which we were dedicated. I know our over-commitment spurred us to some achievements that we wouldn't otherwise have made.

Since then, I have seen many individuals set goals that were higher than I knew they could achieve. I knew they would fail on a few, but I also knew that their net achievement would exceed what they would otherwise do, and that next time they would know better how to scale their goals.

Stretching for tough goals is a great way to learn how good you are, as a person or a team. When you miss a few, you have an exact measurement. If you complete everything, you're never quite sure that you couldn't have done more. Sometimes an underestimated schedule must be made up by working longer hours. Other selected items may be allowed to slip past the original schedule and made up later.

How do you score this kind of play? The primary way is to ask whether you did what you said you would do. Once again, 80 to 90 percent is close to perfect if you included a few risky commitments.

But there's a second measure. You and your supervisor have to consider what you would have accomplished if you had not over-committed. It's a subjective evaluation, but in many cases your over-commitment may have produced far more than if you had not over-committed.

TOLERANCE OF FAILURE

Different people and different organizations have different attitudes toward failure. You have to consider this when you conceive your commitment as well as when you make commitments to others.

Some people play on commitments as a means of motivation, either for themselves or for others. They say a high goal slightly missed may still be a tremendous performance in actual measurement, or as compared with prior performance—for example, "I broke the record by twenty-two seconds, but my goal was to break it by thirty seconds." Few can regard this as failure; but some do.

Differences in attitude toward failure lead to hedging games. You need to be sensitive to the game with your supervisor, and in your organization. In most cases, those attitudes affect how you play your game; can you be candid about your work goals, or must you hedge them down to certainties? Sometimes the attitudes become real obstacles; you can't get the resources or be given the time without an approved commitment.

Assume that your supervisor has a low tolerance for missed goals. You know that you can produce 100 units a month if all goes well.

If things go poorly, you will produce 80 units at best. Should you commit to 80, 90, or 100 units this month? Your answer depends on the failure tolerances of both you and your boss. Each is a good answer under certain conditions.

The low answer, 80 units, seems to be the safe answer. It probably is also the most costly. The high answer, 100 units, looks risky in any case. Your commitment may need more assurance than it offers.

Committing to 90 units, and explaining that possibilities range from 80 to 100 units, may be the best. It takes away some of the heady challenge, but it leaves the 100 goal in sight.

This kind of hedging, with its lack of candor, may be a necessary part of your commitments. Measurable production is an oversimplified illustration, but the considerations apply to more abstract tasks also. Just don't let the hedging game keep you from making challenging commitments to yourself.

SELF-CONTROL

The boss is describing a job that you've been eager to have. You're only half-listening, thinking instead, "This is a piece of cake." Without hesitation, you commit, and you've bitten off more than you can chew. This is a problem of immaturity. How do you handle it?

First, recognize that you have the problem. You're popping off too soon, making commitments without listening. Part of the problem is your enthusiasm. That you must keep.

What you might do is think and plan more before you commit— habitually. Show your enthusiasm for opportunities by listening more and by probing.

Changing habits takes time; what can you do in the meantime? Many things. Read books on related subjects. They tend to be gimmicky, but some of them are good. Design your own approach, including both a change in personal style and an interim technique to embed the habit. It can be no more than a note in your pocket that you read before and after work for a couple of weeks. Leave it there; you may want to check it again for a longer period.

FINDING OUT HOW GOOD YOU ARE

Most people never give any thought to how good they are. Any thoughts they may have on being poorly used usually stem from the pressure of needing more pay. They often work for supervisors very much like themselves. They give no thought to their potential and how they might use it. While they may be somewhat aware that they have a capability for growth, they don't evaluate it.

My concern is that such people are playing a game without realizing it; they're making decisions without knowing it. With their actions, they are determining how their family lives and establishing their future path.

When some of them grasp the idea that their abilities are three to ten times higher than they have been thinking, they're struck with the new possibilities. When they are also offered a simple system for fulfilling their potential, they are doubly intrigued. Then add the idea that their company needs their personal growth as much as they do, and they're ready to do something—but what?

If you're such a person, what can you do? First assume that you have this greater ability. Then experiment—try a few things to see if you can make something different happen for yourself.

Consider the example of a young woman I knew who was ready to break out of a career pattern of secretarial work. When we talked she was about to win a college degree after five intense years of going to college in the evenings. She understood well the unique reinforcement that her job work with budgets, expense reports, and assistance to management had given to her academic accounting studies. But she didn't understand the potential advantage that the same combination gave her in seeking a new career path in her company. She viewed herself as a new college graduate when, in reality, her concurrent academic and job work gave her the equivalent of three to five years of experience.

Not understanding that equivalence was not understanding how good she was. That woman had had career talks with counselors and with people working in the career path that she planned. But she and the others didn't recognize the degree of equivalent experience that her work and school combination had given her.

Together, she and I developed a realistic evaluation of this eye-opener. She made her first job inquiry at a fairly high supervisory level, higher than she would have done on her own. She did it with no introduction. She was surprised at the enthusiastic reception she received.

As she approached the end of her course, I suggested that she consider talking to the vice-president about her primary interest. This seemed audacious to her; she couldn't imagine doing it. But she was intrigued. We discussed the risks and the possible gain, and the tactics she might use. She considered a contrived accidental meeting (cafeteria, hallway, etc.) versus a straightforward request for a brief meeting. She decided on the latter. Before making the request, she organized herself in case she got an immediate response. Again, she couldn't believe how well her interview went. Her meeting with the vice-president was a confirmation of shared needs: her company's, for capable people with initiative;

her own, to feel that she would be needed and well received in the new work that attracted her.

A contact of this type, well executed, will have a lasting significance beyond the small effort involved. Times of major decision and change, such as this person needed, are particularly well suited to an imaginative approach of this type.

This young woman's action filled another need. Many people who earn late academic degrees never fully assume the mantle they have earned. They stay in a similar assignment: same associates, same organization, with pay that is a notch higher. These people never develop the magnitude increase in expectations the new potential for work value justifies.

The young woman in our example went on to unusual growth. She answered the "how good" in a manner that made her do even better. She earned one of the most remarkable pay advances that I have known; in a few years, she earned pay increases greater than an average person earns in a whole career.

My second case of a person learning "How good am I?" is incomplete; it has just started. A young man (thirty-plus) is in his career stride, doing well. But he has only limited understanding of his company's need, his company's potential, and of his potential to fill those opportunities at a much faster pace.

I watched him for a while before I discussed the career game with him. (I'm reluctant to stir expectations until I'm confident that the potential's there.) I commented on a couple of specific things that he had done well. We discussed our views of future opportunities. He was interested but considered the challenges to be out of his league. I mentioned a recent promotion filled by someone whose qualifications approximated his own. He had never talked to, or even met, the supervisor who filled the opening. Why? "You

know, chain of command, jumping levels, and so forth . . ."—
barriers he has created for himself. Handled properly, there is no
obstacle to his knowing—and being known by—people who hand
out opportunities. Incidentally, these are the same people who
need him to succeed.

He got interested; he nibbled at my bait. I talked pay opportunity.
Using public data about pay, we worked out a brief model of the
specific pay progress that comparable people had to be earning.
He did it, but he had a hard time believing the results of his calculations.

This young man had realized that the company's needs and his
capability defined a significantly greater growth than he was experiencing and expecting. We discussed people in higher assignments with qualifications generally comparable to his. His choice:
Wait for this kind of opportunity to come to him, or take action.

Now this man was hooked, but hesitant. That's good. The essence of his problem was that I knew that he was better than he
knew he was. He was ready to experiment, to take limited risk.
We talked tactics, possible ways for him to probe the company, to
test the water, to try himself at the game. He was still hesitant but
still hooked.

Just a week later, all smiles, he described his conversation with
his vice-president. He was exhilarated, but still a little apprehensive. The meeting went well. He couldn't understand one thing:
The VP seemed to think he was asking for a job change. He and I
talked about this and agreed that he could view the VP's comments as indicating the VP had a job he needed to fill. They will
talk again.

This man has just started. He's being careful not to offend his
supervisor or waste the time of his executive. Operating at this

level is new and interesting to him. He is taking action. He is broadening his contacts. It's a novel change for him. He is learning by his *actions* how good he is.

These two cases have similar patterns. First, both of the principals initiated careful actions to test and define their abilities and expand their operation in their company environment. Second, they both learned that they will be well received, and can be comfortable and successful in the process. They will lose a few plays, but I know they can handle that when it happens.

THE LOSER

You can't win 'em all and I've known a couple of losers. One is a man who was interesting because he had let his learning slip. He was middleaged but had given up his go. A new supervisor introduced him to management system concepts and to the basics of data processing. The supervisor also gave him a shot of expectation. It was a real rejuvenation for this man and initiated some good, needed work.

His work section was small; he had the freedom to do whatever work was needed. He tried new things. One symptom of challenging work is people voluntarily working overtime on innovations, and he did a good share of this.

Next, he needed to grow. He identified, went after, and succeeded in getting a new growth assignment. His supervisor hated losing him.

But he blew it!

We had misjudged how good he was. None of us, including him, realized how much he depends on his supervisor's motivation and expectation. With active supervision and suggested ideas, he did a great job. But he wasn't a self-starter; he didn't do it on his own.

Even his failure worked out, but it wouldn't have if he hadn't helped himself. He went after a job of critical, demanding routine, and got it. It's his thing; he does it well.

UNIVERSAL POTENTIAL

Realizing how good you are and what you can do can come like flipping a switch, or reading a book. It is realization. But the realization comes in a package of things:

> I realize I am good. I have the same excellent potential that other good people have. I have to use and develop that good for myself. Other people can help me, both with the realization and the doing. But the responsibility and the capability to develop my good—to be better—is my own.

How much better? Not a little bit better; a lot better—at least 25 to 50 percent or more—and soon!

Until those realizations occur to you, any idea of a system that you can use to double your progress and work satisfaction is inconceivable. Usually, you have never considered that your company might need the same things of you that you need—shared goals, shared achievements.

Even in companies that apply these concepts, most working people have never considered applying ideas like shared goals within their company to personal career needs. However, most managers and supervisors grow with such attitudes and, as they rise, they take the attitudes—shared goals, shared needs—with them.

3

The Company Game

Know it or not, like it or not, the company you're in, or will be in, is a big, fascinating game. Tough or easy, it's a game.

Your momma didn't tell you because she didn't know. If your teachers told you about it, they probably implied that the rules are unfair. (Either elected not to play the game, or lost out if they did.)

There are always magazine and newspaper articles saying what's wrong with this game and its rules. But of the 100 million of us who play in the United States alone, most go home with a reasonable amount of satisfaction and the pay that goes with it.

This game is not trivial. This game has rules. This game has tactics and strategies. Prizes can be won by all. Your prizes, your success, your winnings depend on your understanding the game—your tactics, your strategies, but mostly how effectively you use yourself during the workday.

THE COMPANY'S PLAN FOR YOU

Forget it! Your company has no plans or goals for you, and there won't be any unless you make them. And there isn't any "The Company." It's just not a part of the game!

Many people think that some omnipotent executive has created, and maintains, the master plan for their careers. There's no such person or thing. Your supervisor is your closest connection with your company. As you make your plans, use your supervisor for help and let him or her know that you expect that help.

You don't have to pour out your heart. If you intend to be president, hold off telling your supervisor. Just take a little of his or her time now to help you for the next six to twelve months.

Would you want it any other way? Do you realize that surrendering your career management to your company would be surrendering your personal freedom? Decide for yourself what you want to do and go after it!

YOUR SITUATION—COMPANY AND YOU

The shops, the desks, and the halls of your company are filled with people working far below their ability, below their potential. These people can do far better work than they do today. Is this some kind of Communist Manifesto? Quite the opposite! This is the rankest kind of capitalist exhortation! If you don't raise yourself and fulfill more of your potential, you and your company both lose. My call for action is to you, not your company.

Management knows that its employees are working far below their potential, that the primary limitation to the company's success and growth is the sum of the limitations that each person places on his or her personal growth.

But management is limited in what it can say. I am not. We—the company and its management—need your success. Take the initiative to understand the goals that you and your company share, and work for your goals.

THE GAME ATTITUDE

Developing the game attitude is a top-notch way to understand the real workings of your company. It has major advantages:

It forces you to recognize the real rules and customs of your company's game. You see with new eyes how it operates, its organization, and the styles of the people with whom you work, particularly your managers and supervisors.

You begin to simulate and model your career actions. You visualize moves that you design to advance you from your present assignment to an attractive career goal. You anticipate your problems early enough to develop solutions. You can compare alternative approaches.

You can eliminate or minimize risks associated with your personal plans.

Consider how you learn a new game. Look at the game in your company as three steps:

Understand how the game is played.

Plan the career game that you will play.

Execute—play your game.

STEP 1—UNDERSTANDING THE GAME

Figure 3.1 graphically portrays two important phases of the game in your company: understanding the game and planning your game. This approach assumes that you have a basic understanding of company objectives, goals, types of products, and so forth. The rest of this chapter discusses the first step—understanding the game. Planning your game is discussed in later chapters. And playing your game is, of course, for you to write.

Some of your company's rules are real no-nos; they're absolute. These include a series of don'ts. You don't drink, fight, give or take bribes, or make sexual advances at work. The penalty is dismissal. There aren't many absolutes and they're not our interest here.

The less rigid rules and customs are vital to our game. Many practices accepted as rules are, in fact, only customs. You can carefully test these; you may find just the opportunity you want hidden behind a custom.

FIGURE 3.1. Approach to the game.

Consider an example. The VP-Personnel is just five years from retirement. Executive jobs in Personnel have always been filled by someone who has grown up in the ranks of Personnel. This is generally accepted as a rule.

Your background includes a great deal of experience in manufacturing supervision and education in engineering. You have been frustrated for several years because of inadequate support from Personnel. You are recognized as having furnished some of your own personnel support when you needed it.

You are in a strong position to make yourself a candidate for the VP-Personnel job. A custom that many people regard as a rule would appear to be almost an invitation for you to become the next VP-Personnel. You need to model several plans that might take you to this goal. This probably will take you at least a couple of weeks. One approach may be a direct one to the present VP. You're not asking to be tagged heir-apparent; you just want to be a candidate. The VP might be interested in a gradual shift of his or her load to a strong candidate. This has to be done cautiously.

As you design each of the several plans to which you may want to commit, consider alternatives that you might have to use in case of failure. These may be either for the whole approach or for some tactical part of the plan.

NEXT OPENING IS YOURS

"Next opening is yours" is a common custom that most organizations might not recognize they follow: if you make a good, strong, proper, qualified bid for a new job, and fail, you will be offered the next good opening for which you are qualified.

This custom often operates in career management situations. I have seen it work many times. In one case, someone whom I had worked with was crushed and depressed when he lost a well-managed job bid. The job was given to another person who had actively sought the job. I told him that he would be offered an equivalently attractive opportunity within eight to ten weeks. It happened; it almost always happens.

These customs tend to cluster together. Consider this case and the case of the person bidding for the VP-Personnel job. First, in Personnel, it is customary to promote from within. Second, these two situations indicate that career mobility and self-help are encouraged. Third, they may also imply that best-person-for-the-job takes priority over promotion from within. Fourth, if the next-opening principle works, the likelihood for a good job is high when your first bid fails (thus a soft failure). Fifth, the overall climate for managing your own career is good.

Since all of these rules can affect a simple case, it is apparent that a large, mature company may have many rules and customs. Further, it's apparent that most of these rules and customs are not written or even recognized by many people. Most who work with these rules and customs are not even aware that they're operating, though in many cases, they control peoples' destinies. If you never take time to recognize what the game is, and continue to use many of the rules and customs intuitively, you will fail to take advantage of others because you won't be aware of them. Some are actually acting against you and can be turned to your advantage if you understand them. Awareness of the rules and customs, written and unwritten, is an essential part of developing the habit of looking for opportunity.

Consider an outright negative rule. Few are more common or destructive than limitations of personal movement based on levels of formal education or your field of education. You can overcome this type of barrier if you recognize it and deliberately plan for it. There are several ways; some are almost like formulas. Look for people who have already overcome the barriers; use them as models; try doing what they did. But do so without explicitly claiming that fairness requires that you be given the same freedom as X.

Perhaps the one best way to overcome a custom is the Try Me tactic. Watch for an opening—someone goes on vacation, people are needed to work overtime, and so forth. Move in with Try Me—"Try me in this work; I need to learn and you need me to learn."

You must also be alert not to let the positive rules work against you. If you're in Personnel and expected a crack at that VP-Personnel job, you may view our hero as an interloper. If the custom in your company is that jobs go to the best qualified, regardless of prior experience, you'd better use your opportunity and experience to qualify yourself. Handled properly, you should have the inside track to the job.

The rules of the game in most companies would fill a book. It would have to be an ever-changing book to keep up with the evolution of new customs. But the lack of formal documentation is extremely valuable to you and your company. It's essential to the freedom and flexibility both you and your company need.

In the career game, few things are more interesting than the interplay among normal rules and customs. Consider three broad areas: pay, job mobility, and personal customs.

PAY CUSTOMS

Pay customs affect you even before you report to work. An increase that you negotiate during your hiring process may still affect your pay five years later. However, the better you do in your work, the less effect your starting pay will have on your continuing pay. And, selecting your company based on a starting pay offer may be one of your worst decisions.

There's nothing wrong with questioning your recruiter as to the pay practices in the company. The recruiter may flinch and suggest that you can't understand until you come into the company. Tell him: "Try me."

Consider an executive I know who, when being recruited from school, routinely asked his recruiters about their pay and the kind of increases his recruiters were experiencing. He says that it surprised them but didn't seem to hurt his chances.

Chapter 11 discusses the concepts of pay structure. Using them, you can sketch a simple model of the actual pay structure in your company. You can find where specific jobs fit into the pay structure, and use this as a map on which to sketch the route you want to follow.

In some companies it is taboo to ask for a pay raise. In others, you have to ask. Most companies and most supervisors are receptive to your personal goals and expectations. Even if your supervisor is reluctant, this kind of discussion, conducted carefully, teaches you about the pay system, how the company applies it, and how your supervisor passes out his or her raise money. If you have to ask to get a raise, you want to convince your supervisor that the value of your work has increased, is increasing, and will continue to increase. Never base a request for an increase on the rising cost of living.

SUPERVISORS' STYLES

Understanding and using your supervisor's style is a major determinant of your career progress. It affects how your supervisor uses you, how you use your supervisor, how much you learn, and how much and how fast you develop. For now, briefly consider how your supervisor fits into your world of career management.

It is easy to work with and benefit from a supervisor who has a positive style. An example is an operating manager whose style is to make active use of his controller and the control function. When a financial review is planned, he sketches what he wants and expects you to produce a good draft three days before the presentation. He makes minor revisions, adds a couple of requirements, and you give it to the graphics section. Finished copy is ready the day before the presentation, and you've had maximum opportunity for personal initiative.

But you can develop yourself as much or more working for a supervisor who has a negative style. You can learn to use tactics complementary to such a supervisor's style. Consider the exact opposite of the preceding case. Ignore for the moment the simple power the supervisor has over you. He has some positive contribution to offer; regardless of the supervisor's negative elements, he has some combination of knowledge, experience, and access to upper levels that you need. Your thinking goes like this: My supervisor has little use for me or my control function. But this is contrary to the custom of our company. He's a seat-of-the-pants manager in a tightly controlled company. Whether he likes it or not, he needs me, and I need him.

You couldn't ask for a better opportunity. The burden's on you, but you can make your shared needs a beautiful combination! The supervisor needs your support and you need acceptance and participation as his controller. Your solution lies in shaping your personal style and tactics to compensate for his. Work with his operating managers to solve your common control problem, and use these people to reach him. They share your problem. They recognize their need for control support and for your success. Train them; get them to use you; and they will sell you to your common supervisor. This is no behind-the-back deal. Done in the open, everyone gains; the big chief has a well-controlled operation, and his operating managers learn and improve their control. You will turn the negative style of your supervisor to your joint, positive benefit.

This is typical of situations where you do more than just compensate for negative factors; instead, you use such problems as a positive handle for progress.

HOW TO USE YOUR COMPANY'S GAME

Assume that your company follows a basic policy that salaried people must have college degrees. You don't have a degree, but you intend to become salaried and to continue earning pay raises after you do. Or you have the same kind of ambitions and you have a degree in history or education in a company of salespeople, engineers, and accountants.

How do you play the game under these circumstances and succeed? Remember, to succeed, both you and your company must share your success.

First, look around and learn just how the game is really played in your company. This may not be easy. It's information that you want; you may want to look and listen very quietly. You want to find the cracks and crevices, the handholds for yourself in the scheme of things. The exceptions that you're looking for tend to cluster in selected areas. Be careful.

You spot a couple of salaried people who bear the "good'ol'boy" label. These are people, perhaps not so old, who are good in their jobs. One is a fellow in the shop who used to be a technician for the president when the president was an engineer. Another is a supervisor who runs the night shift in data processing. Others include a manager and two supervisors in maintenance. None of these great people has a degree, and the realities of their situations express the real policy.

You can keep looking, but you may have enough information to understand some major and minor patterns of both your company and the people who have broken this barrier. Before you try to understand this part of the game and its tactics, consider the reason for the rule.

As a general rule, most companies agree that their best people in management and professional work have college degrees related to their assignments. The correlation is good, but there are many exceptions.

There are people trained as lawyers and accountants who are executives of companies of high-techology products, or products dependent on success in mass marketing. There are a few who rose from the bench to manage the company. Oddly enough, most of these are now backers of the rule for having a degree to be salaried.

Sorting out the backgrounds for success, there are some common characteristics. One is that these people have knowledge, or know how to get it. This is the most recognized characteristic of college graduates. Another less-recognized characteristic is that most *college graduates know how to set and seek goals*. This is something that most people entering work directly from high school do not have. In college, you must develop some of this goal-setting, goal-seeking capability for yourself.

Now return to the people you identified without degrees. Generally, they all have fair knowledge of their work and they have basic knowledge of how to set and achieve goals. They may not think of themselves that way, but that's one of the primary means they used to break the barrier. Having these two characteristics, they are competitive with college graduates.

But there's more. They may be better qualified for certain jobs. Most of them have experienced prolonged vertical growth. They have performed in many of the jobs they now manage; they have worked closely with many others. Further, their jobs may not be attractive to many college graduates. Maintenance is an on-call, round-the-clock job to keep the plant working, even if it's not a multishift plant. Data processing operations supervisors are subject to twenty-four-hour call. The payroll operation is vital to both morale and legal requirements. Its supervision requires high quality performance to exacting standards.

As you look over these game patterns, you search other areas and functions and understand the game. So in a company where only 15 to 20 percent of salaried people don't have degrees, you can spot pockets where 50 percent or more don't have degrees.

But you have to dig out this kind of information, or recognize the patterns of information you have previously ignored. Then you have to understand the game that it implies. Never mind what the stated policy says. In many companies even the powers-that-be don't recognize some of the real rules and policies of their games.

Does one of these areas interest you? If it does, can you design plays and tactics to play on that field? For instance, if most of the incumbents broke the barrier at age thirty-two, can you design a game to break the barrier at age twenty-six or twenty-eight?

JOB MOBILITY CUSTOMS

Customs of job mobility influence both your career path and pace. Therefore, both your personal style and your tactics are affected.

Some companies post their job openings internally. This may work to your personal disadvantage if you are active in seeking your own job openings. It may work to the company's advantage because so few people actively seek their own job openings. It promotes a pervasive feeling that opportunity is automatic if people will just use the advantages pointed out to them.

Before you depend on this rule, check how it's applied. Notices of vice-presidential openings are rare. There must be other openings that are not announced, some level where openings are not up for grabs. Are there other qualifications? There must be. There have to be rules of urgency, security of company information, and so forth. These commonly result in a reasonable custom: *Many of the most attractive jobs are usually filled before the opening is announced.* So if there is any job that you want, let the right person know it well before that job opens up. Never assume that you are next in line, or that you will automatically be a candidate for the job that you want.

Mobility customs apply even when you are leaving your company. No company can beg you to stay; that would invite blackmail. However, if you have a firm offer and if you are recognized as unusually valuable, you can make the *velvet threat* one time, carefully: "I have an offer too attractive for me not to consider. I owe it to my family to consider it. You have been so good to me that I feel obligated to let you know before I . . . ." I know someone who parlayed this situation into an immediate vice-presidency of a small company without leaving his desk.

PERSONAL CUSTOMS

I have worked for two great companies. Both are shirt-sleeve, first-name, companies; clothing is respectable, but casual; people are addressed by their first names regardless of level. Both customs invite communication and collaboration based simply on common need and shared goals. Both tend to remove barriers between people. They are pervasive, personal invitations to communications and interrelations.

Many people forget the magnitude of the name barrier. Young people and people from modest backgrounds are reluctant to call forty- to sixty-year-olds Harry, or Mary, or John. They have been raised to say Mister, or Missis, or Sir. This is often a source of personal discomfort on both sides, and I have urged many young people to break this barrier early.

I work with a young man who had this problem. In our informal environment he addressed me as "Sir." I explained the barrier he created with this practice, and that it was a part of other personal habits that tended to isolate him. He revised some of his habits; he said that some were hard to change but that peoples' reactions made the change interesting. This smacks a little of prostitution, but I consider it a reasonable modification of personal style. (You don't get invited to dinner if you eat your peas with your knife.) He has retained his reserved personality but is much more relaxed and has an improved presence.

Differences in language illustrate double standards in personal customs. Obscenity, profanity, and other pithy language is used in some presences and places and not in others. These minor differences don't bother me. Job opportunities and meaningful privileges do—we can't permit double standards in these. Our progress in these customs and styles are a true social revolution.

You can easily list twenty to fifty personal customs of people or groups of even a modest-sized company. Some, such as ethics, refusing job transfers, and freedom of personal communications, are major determinants of the tone of a company. It is worth your time to recognize the customs that affect you and the ones that you can use to help you manage your career.

The players' styles are as important to your game as the rules and customs. Actual practice is a mixture of actions that move well outside the customs and others that fail to use the opportunities that customs offer. Actual practice changes the customs themselves. Most of this is good and tends to control the deadwood. Some of it takes us into bad territory.

But this tendency of the company, or a work group, to adopt the changes pressed on it by people is a rich opportunity that you can use for your personal development. Not only can you use it to shape and develop your personal style, you can be a significant influence on how your company works.

There are innumerable variations of personal style, and infinite combinations of them. Chapter 7 expands on this. If you could see yourself, you'd be more surprised than you would by hearing your recorded voice. Your habits at work, use of voice, social contacts, lunch companions, reactions to challenges, levels of acquaintances, good-ol'-boy, aggressiveness, persistence, workhorse, personal organizations, Try Me, and so on, are all major components of your career.

Consider briefly an illustration of personal styles in the relations between a woman and her supervisor. (Chapter 13 expands this subject.) This description of one problem and its solution illustrates the general approach to taking personal styles into account: defining what you want, identifying others who have overcome similar problems, adapting their solutions to your problem, your environment, and your style. You even want to do a similar thing better for yourself. It's intriguing; it's really a game!

The woman was a young secretary-clerk whom I commended for effectively answering my questions on a complex administrative problem. (My normal source, an older, salaried person, was out sick.) We talked about her career. She told me of her intention to stay with our company in her present job for six or seven more years (a total of fifteen), then leave to get a higher, salaried job in the same field with another company. I'm always challenged when a valuable person, someone with potential, has this kind of plan — particularly if they're in my company.

Think of all the career waste this person was planning both for herself and our company. Think of all the opportunity to which she had blinded herself! She was giving up the opportunity of some of the best years of her career. Why? She had let herself be discouraged by her supervisor; he had told her that she couldn't become salaried unless she earned a degree. She wouldn't pay that price given her family situation.

Yet the contradiction to her supervisor's "policy" was all around her. The salaried person with whom I normally talk had no degree; the young woman knew it. We discussed several other women who held salaried jobs despite not having degrees. Some she knew about; she was surprised to learn about others and how many there were. She had not read an article in our employee paper that mentioned that between 15 and 20 percent of our salaried people didn't have degrees.

We talked of the possible approaches she could take, of ways to overcome this barrier. How long would it take her to define a goal and make a plan? She had good basic qualifications; it's hard to believe she couldn't become salaried in two years. How?

Her present job was a knowledge job and a math job, and she had the background and inclination for both. She understood much of the information passing through her hands, but with more interest, she could become expert in it, for example, by reading publications in the field.

How about her political situation? This was a much tougher problem. She had made it tougher already by accepting her supervisor's "policy." This problem was best left alone while she developed herself for more valuable work. She agreed that there were many opportunities for higher-level initiative that she had not been using. I reminded her that each time one of her initiatives is accepted, overtly or tacitly, it would be a recognition of the growth and value of her work. Even her errors, if kept in reasonable control, would contribute to her learning and value. The one barrier that she did not have to overcome was inability. I look forward to talking to this woman again soon. She was challenged by the game concept; I felt she would play it and succeed.

You can use negative supervisors and situations as spurs and opportunities; turn them around to your positive benefit.

SCORING THE GAME

There are two kinds of success and a scoring system for each. Your external success tends to be scored on the basis of money and material gain, except by your family and friends.

Your personal career success must be measured by you. Of its two parts—satisfying work and pay—you are almost the sole scorekeeper of the first. I rank pay as a major scoring factor, as I said in Chapter 1; after a year or so it expresses the value that your company assigns to your work.

To both of these measurements you must add the prime personal measurement discussed in Chapter 2: Do you do what you say you will do? An 80 to 90 percent answer to this question is a nearly perfect score in the career game.

IS THIS REALLY THE GAME?

I am neither blind nor a fool. I know that what I've described doesn't always work that way. I know that some companies do it wrong. I know that in companies that do it right there are some supervisors and managers who do it wrong. I know that people get hurt to the point where they will neither try nor risk anything.

However, there is nearly always some way, some crevice that you can use, to start yourself on the road to success in your company's game. There is always somebody—at work, at home, at your place of worship—who will help you.

I was invited to speak to a group of students whom my company was recruiting. I was allowed to speak freely, but I qualified my views as being my own. I shot it to them: "This is the way the career game is played: The responsibility for your career development is your own. I hate to admit it, but you can win the game this way in any good company."

The students were active in both discussions and challenges. The next day one student asked, "Is it really that way in your company?" I wish, instead, he had asked, "Can I really make it that way in your company?"

4

You're Making It Sound Too Simple!

Oh, but it is simple! I'm not speaking of a roaring turnaround and charging off in a new direction tomorrow. I am speaking of a considered decision six weeks from now and progress from then on.

The change is a dawning, a realization: "Oh, is *that* the way the game is played? I can do that!" The change I'm offering you is not new; you've experienced the same kind of change before. Think of when you learned to drive, draw a picture, ride a bicycle, ski, swim, skate, or play the guitar. Remember how it seemed impossible at first, but that at some point you suddenly developed an understanding of the basic concepts. After that, it came naturally.

Sound familiar? What was your own problem that you solved so simply when you finally understood the game? The career game works that same, simple way.

There's more to the change than just "I can do it," but it's just as simple. It is your conscious agreement with that voice inside you that says, "I am meant for more than this. I am meant to keep growing. What I am now, and what I have now, is not all that is meant for me. There is more for me and I can make it happen." This is a purely selfish thought but its fulfillment implies continual contributions by you to others.

This is your plan for *you*. Only you can do it. Inevitably, you get other ideas at first: "I will get someone else to do it with me," or "I will get someone to help me make the initial commitment." No way! *You must make the decision yourself*. After that you may get help setting your goals.

THE SIMPLE WAY

Regardless of how you choose to play your career game, you start the same way: You decide to do it.

After your decision, recognize that you are committing to sustain actions to achieve more with your personal potential. At this point, you're ready for your next decision. Consider the sequence of steps and alternatives that this decision starts:

Decide and Commit. "I will sustain actions to achieve more of my potential in my career. In a nutshell, I'm going for more challenging work, and more money."

Next Decision. "Will I go the full goal-seeking route, or simply start on a series of brief career-improvement projects?" If you need to build a little confidence to start, take the easy second path. If, instead, you are ready for the goal-seeking route, start out that way; prepare for the one hard part—developing your initial goals.

Develop Initial Goals. Don't expect this to be easy. Chances are strong that you'll have to struggle a few weeks to develop a goal for three to eight years. It's worth the effort. Remember that these are *work* goals, no go-back-to-school stuff at first. You'll probably modify or change these original goals later; that doesn't matter. For now you have attractive goals with which to start your planning.

Start Planning. Sketch the milestones and actions to get to your goals, but concentrate on the near-term actions. You're ready to start your new game when you're clear on the actions you're going to take in the next few weeks to change your work.

SPOTTING OPPORTUNITY

Where is your opportunity? Depending on how choosy you are, everywhere. If your heart is set on a field like drawing and illustration, you have defined a narrow field for yourself. Stick to it if that's what you want, but it's a tough way to start. You could still get close to your goal, if you broadened your field to graphics in general. You would have something to feed the kitty while you start, and you would stand a higher probability of working close to your chosen field. This may be a compromise, a postponement, or simple recognition that you can't get exactly what you want now.

For most of my career, I have known what I want, but from the very first, I have encountered, or been offered, jobs quite different from what I wanted. I nearly always accepted the alternative and have never regretted the choice.

Deep inside, many people just want to join a good group, do useful work, and have an opportunity to grow and advance. That's good. Often, those who have these feelings won't recognize or accept them, feeling that they should have a strong dedication to some field or some job. That just isn't necessary.

Now, however, contrast this idea with my proposed approach to a job: go after a particular job. If someone suggests an alternative, consider it. If you will work with good people, do satisfying work, and have an opportunity to grow, that particular job is for you, for now.

Some career fields require specialized education or training—law, medicine, and engineering are typical. Without the educational background, you have a slim chance of growing in these fields. They may be ideal if you intend to get the necessary education.

But opportunity knocks. You can spot rewarding, important fields not normally associated with specific formal training. Don't misunderstand me; I'm not saying these fields don't require knowledge and education. They do. However, a more general background is often acceptable.

Consider *purchasing*. People who buy for a business do work far more important than is generally recognized. Part of the reason for limited formal courses in the field may be that we have less understanding of the personal arts that make up much of the purchasing work. In many manufacturing businesses, one-half of the price of products represents goods purchased. Effective purchasing is an obvious key to costs, but it can be equally important to quality and delivery schedules. Management knows this far better than is generally recognized. Yet there are no generally accepted formal qualifications for this work. If negotiation arts are attractive to you and you can correlate them with your company's operations, purchasing is an important career field that is available to you. Because it is a critical occupation, there are local qualifications for entry to its various jobs.

If you explore this kind of work to learn the game in your company, try to understand which qualifications are founded on a solid basis and which tend to be capricious. This has a significant bearing on how you play your game.

THE ONE HARD PART

The single hard part of the career game is developing your first goal, deciding for the first time what you want and will work for. My first time was like a flash; I realized in just a few moments a change in direction that I wanted to make, a field in which I had had no previous interest. The second time, I saw a memo that described a new organization in a challenging field. In both cases, I immediately began planning to find a way. It worked both times.

These are the lucky, easy kind. I see them happen about one-third of the time. The others can be a real struggle and they take longer. I'm convinced that the first step is to set your date: "Six weeks from now, I will set a goal, start my plan." I have not worked with anyone who has made the commitment and not ended with a goal. But I have worked with quite a few who have never committed.

THE BIG DIFFERENCE

I have been baffled by the reluctance of some people to decide and commit on a career approach. I thought they were just procrastinating. Then I realized what a big obstacle it can be. I also know that the problem may be a continuing misunderstanding between some supervisors and the people whom they're trying to help with career planning. If you have this problem, your solution is illustrated by the examples I used at the opening of this chapter—find the success pattern with which you started your career, just as you found the success pattern for a game or other challenge.

The reason that some supervisors have a hard time understanding your problem in making a career-approach decision is that they have already developed or acquired a simple approach to solutions and decisions and may not even be aware of their system. Here is their simple approach:

They review and define their problem. They involve their people. But in the end, they make the best decision they can. They commit to perform and ask their people for the same commitment. But they know that their decisions are arbitrary. They don't search for a magic key to a problem; they know that there is no single, ordained solution, no guarantee of success. Instead, they hope they're choosing the best path. In any case, they hope that by committing to that path and its goal they will make it happen.

I don't know whether most managers and supervisors struggled or even suffered to learn this process of decision making. I don't know whether their first decisions were painful. I don't mean to be saying that many decisions they make now are not painful. I do know that the process is easier for them, and they accept the arbitrary nature of many of their decisions no matter how firmly they seem to have been made.

Until I realized how difficult the original career decision and commitment is for some people, I had a major barrier in helping them make their first career steps. Many supervisors have this same barrier. If you have the problem, take steps to solve it.

Use some of the manager's approach if you are reluctant to make your first career decision and commitment. Your decision will be simpler if you remember that the distant goal you select can be changed as you learn to play the game. When you work down to the near-term actions that you must start with, design simple moves that you feel confident of achieving. If they're trivial, don't worry. They're probably good starters; keep them to yourself and make the next ones more significant.

THE POSTPONERS

You may think you don't have the problem I've just described. If you have trouble getting started, see if you have either of the following two common symptoms; when I first encountered them, I thought they were simple procrastination (people just wanting to talk and not really wanting to manage their careers). But that's not true; the symptoms indicate two real problems.

>   *Number One Postponer*. People inexperienced in the goal-seeking method are unwilling to commit to do something that they don't know yet how to do.

>   *Number Two Postponer*. People don't want to select a job goal three to five years away without understanding all of the jobs available.

The first problem is like a fear of the unknown. Some people who have this problem are the strong, aggressive type. I don't yet have an effective pattern solution, or formula, for solving this problem. The best approach I know is to observe the people performing jobs near you that are attractive to you.

These people are not water-walkers; they are not miracle-makers. Their work is a little different from yours; it may be a level higher, but a year or so ago they were probably dong the same work you're doing now. If you discuss their work with them, they will be surprised that you consider it challenging. A few, usually the insecure, may try to talk up their jobs, making them seem more difficult than they are, but most people will assure you that you will learn their work quickly when you get the opportunity and responsibility.

The second problem has some of the same easy solutions. You just don't need to know about all jobs to get started. Learn and understand the closely related jobs at first, jobs both at the same level and immediately above your own work. Talk to people. Volunteer to fill in during their absences. But be careful again; insecure people may regard you as a threat.

Becoming familiar with these new jobs solves your problems of setting near-term goals. Just choose one that interests you as your near-term goal.

Choosing your first long-term goal is just as simple. If you're having a hard time on the first one, just assume that you will advance vertically. This means that your present planning will be modeled on getting your boss's job, and then his or her boss's job, and, after that, who knows?

If you take this route for the present, you have a simple solution. It puts you in the planning business; you have started learning to manage your career game. You have an interim solution, a reasonable default. Now start looking around, understanding other jobs, other careers. Confirm that you like the decisions that you've made, or decide to change.

You may have a more difficult problem—disliking your present work. If you do, don't even make a tentative plan to grow in the same work. That would just lengthen the planning process for you. Begin your search for other fields.

This decision doesn't change my assertion that the game is simple. At least you've started with a decision, at least you're starting a personal movement toward career success.

DO IT NOW!

I hope I've taken away your reasons for postponement. Commit yourself to personal change; set a date now. If you are going the goal-seeking route, plan to create your first goal in six weeks. If you are not going for the whole system, set a date by which you will develop a tactic or two, simple near-term plans to change your work.

As a minimum, determine that you will use your company's performance review procedure to increase the value of your work and pay. If you work in a very small company, or have no regular review, try to influence your supervisor to work with you on some regular basis.

THE OBSTACLES

There are two kinds of career obstacles. Most of them are the kind that we create for ourselves. The others are real obstacles.

Many of the real obstacles can be overcome. Others are unconquerable; you'll just have to find a way around them or not go that route. An example of a real obstacle results from law. Assume that you are a whiz at cutting and dressing hair. You've done your family's and friends', and maybe even been paid by them. Now you want to change your career to hair stylist. You can't do it. The law in your state requires that you successfully complete 1,000 hours of training at an approved school and pass a test. Regardless of your skill and practical knowledge, you must fulfill this requirement or you can't play the game—that's the rule.

The self-created obstacles can seem just as real. I've illustrated several of them already: The postponer's problems are two common ones. Another that I see often has multiple forms; all are based on "they" being against "me." I know people who have worked in several companies, and they all seem to take "they" with them: "'They' seem dedicated to preventing 'my' success. The company is in turmoil and only I have the obvious solution, but 'they' will not listen. Frequently, I have written a memo, addressed three levels up, but all it did was aggravate the ['my'] problem."

To some degree this is a problem for all of us. In a few cases it reflects a genuinely unfair situation. But in most cases it is simply the sorehead who has magnified common minor irritants or magnified his or her own ability to solve pervasive problems.

EVERYONE WANTS TO HELP!

Well, nearly everyone. Even people who need you will help you leave the company if it helps your career. I don't know why; I don't think they know why. It's another common act of grace.

For the most radical change I made in my career, I needed a chain of four people to help me. I planned to convince each that the major change that I wanted was good for both our company and me. I spoke to them in sequence. Each was surprised. They were willing to listen. Each volunteered in turn to pick up my project for me and carry it to completion.

I had anticipated this. I knew that it was my responsibility to sell the change. I asked only for their concurrence and to allow me to carry it up the line.

Their collective cooperation was typical of the help I've seen offered to people making changes. Their offers of excessive help were also typical.

Because these are typical reactions, you must be prepared to control your own show.

Sometimes the help offered you may take a different, dangerous tact, such as an offer from a new company. A young man in my company received an unsolicited, change-companies, 25-percent-pay-increase offer. He was hungry, inexperienced, and flattered, but he wasn't ready. For a year he had improved and he knew it; he was feeling his oats. But he overestimated his pace of improvement. He had already made a tentative decision to change companies when he talked with me. I explained that the decision had to be his but that he was just overcoming some major problems in self-confidence. He chose to stay and was soon drawn into an excellent advancement.

All of the help so generously given you is in support of decisions made by you. I have observed that supervisors typically shy away from helping their people determine basic goals. They seem to be saying, "You must decide that part of your life. You can get counseling, but the initiative, the ideas, must come from you."

A NOT-SO-SIMPLE CASE

I know that not all solutions are simple. I present the following not-so-simple case of a woman subjected to great frustration, who continued to work as if a solution would come. She needed some luck to break the barrier, but she was more than ready when the time came.

This woman grew up expecting to have to work. And she had the multiple motivations of a woman supporting a family with growing kids: she needed the money, she knew she could do a higher level of work, she wanted recognition, and she wanted the door for further opportunity to be explicitly open.

She was on the night shift when I met her. It was a new assignment for me. I visited with the shifts in operation and spoke with each group. No shrinking violet, this woman responded immediately to my call for questions. She had laid her plans well. She had proven her capability by what I think of as the "Tactic of Insinuation." The job she wanted was a notch above her basic work. What was more important, and she knew it, was that it was the first rung of a natural ladder of progression.

The obstacle to women for this job—a semivalid one—was that moderate lifting was required. In reality, for many women of stamina this barrier was obsolete. This woman had used every opportunity to fill in and actually do the work. On her breaks, she had operated the complex equipment. The male operators had come to use her as a substitute—just what she wanted. They knew their job excluded women because of the lifting. But this woman did it all—operating and lifting. She was not to be denied, but she had been denied.

She was ready for me when I asked for questions. I know she expected argument and trouble from me; she had experienced it before. But she, by having tried the work, had made my job easy. There was no decision I had to make. If she got medical approval for the lifting, she had qualified herself for the next opening.

She made it easy for her supervisor to give her the job. No person, in fairness, could have denied her the job she wanted. Call it a plan, call it a scheme—she worked it right. A little risk, but only a little. It could have worked differently. She could have been put off. She could have been denied to the point of having to appeal higher. None of these could-have-beens happened; with only a little delay and a little luck, it all worked out because she was moving on a plan. The two elements of career success were hers. No matter that she didn't view career management as I offer it to you. With her style, with her luck, we all won.

IT IS SIMPLE!

Changing to this bonus route is just as simple as the route you're following now. This good route simply makes you define the achievements that you will reach for and perform tomorrow—the days, weeks, months, and years ahead. It's no more than a personal habit that you create and practice. As you achieve these minor miracles, you will build your personal expectations—what you expect of yourself. The tasks that you set for yourself are no more than anticipating how you will use your personal potential that would otherwise never be developed, never be used.

The other route, the one that nearly all of us follow, is neither harder nor easier. You do the work of today, you achieve, you learn, you have satisfaction. But later, at age thirty, forty or fifty, you look back and say to yourself, "Why have I grown and achieved less than I expected when I started?"

The answer to less-than-hoped-for achievement will lie in how you build your expectations. The positive expectation is hope overlaid with commitment to do something. You have to furnish the motivation, and practice the simple habit now.

5

Succeeding With Expectations

Like many people, I was succeeding with expectations long before I understood their existence and their power. I had the great fortune to start my career with a good supervisor, in a good company, with good management. Our work group was made up of good people with moderate expectations.

But our manager had high expectations and high goals, for the group and for us as individuals. His supervisors caught the excitement from him—it was contagious. (Note that I didn't say high hopes because there's a difference between hope and expectation.) You didn't have to be in the group long before you knew we could do it—that's expectation. We had tough goals. When we started on a new one, we might not know *how* to do it, but we knew that we *would* do it.

I don't mean to paint a fantasy of superpeople just waiting for the spark. We weren't. We were just young, hungry, and fairly capable. We had a sprinkling of seasoned experience and there was respectful banter between the hot-to-trot types and the seasoned ones. To this day I stand in awe of what we accomplished—an extraordinary performance by ordinary people. Expectation was a major element of the power at work.

What was going on among us? First, we had a manager with a goal and a plan. Not a static goal and plan, but an evolving, growing thing that we could all join and contribute to.

We had communication and discussion, between and within levels. With this communication we transmitted the expectation. My primary channel was my supervisor, a real prince. He was literally a disciple in the sense that he understood the discipline we were practicing and passed it on to us. He was a coach; he both taught and motivated us.

It sounds odd, but we had freedom. We knew what was expected and we understood the bounds of behavior, but they were never so narrow that there wasn't constant need for innovation, for invention. We were expected to grow and we did. Some opportunity for growth came from company growth, but much of our growth came because we were recognized as a source of good people. Some of us were requested by other organizations; others left for new opportunities; others came back into our fold as our manager expanded his control.

Since that original job, I've participated in the magic of group expectation several times. I have been a participant as it changed the lives of people and companies. I have been a spectator in other cases. Look into my example for the patterns of expectation that it expresses and implies.

PATHS OF EXPECTATION

Change the locale and the participants from my illustration and you have a typical picture of great expectation working. Look inside and trace the paths of its flow.

Three paths are obvious. Our manager passed his expectation to the whole group. He sparked the supervisors, but he also got to us directly by means of group contact. Our supervisors sustained the most important transfer of expectation. Each of us received continual contact with his or her supervisor. The third path was the lateral support among the peer group; we constantly discussed our projects.

The other two paths of expectation are the least recognized and can be the most valuable to you. The first of these is expectation that goes upward. You can convey to your supervisor, and managers above, what you expect. "Do you mean little ol' me can influence what 'they' do?" That's exactly what I mean! And I mean that your managers ("they") are hungry for you to take a bigger hand. I have already illustrated this with the man who designed his own plan for next year, his performance review, and his pay raise. That's one good example of a person shaping the expectation of those above. The same tool can be applied to many cases, for many purposes. Part of its effectiveness is that so few people dare to use it.

The last path of expectation is within yourself. If your supervisor and your manager can reach you with expectation, you can create your own expectations for yourself.

Now pause and organize these things that you know about expectation. None of this is new to you. I only ask you to organize what you already know. My objectives are two-fold: First, to convince you that you have the power to create expectation and to make it happen for yourself; second, to convince you to use this upward expectation—at the least to influence your supervisor's expectation of you, but more so to consider trying to influence how your company does the kind of work you do.

Most of the things we do, we do because of expectation. We neither hesitate nor doubt. We don't act because of punitive sanctions. Our parents, families, and teachers implanted these expectations. They work. They work so effectively that they continue to give us a routine and assurance. Think of our early years. We were told what to do and how to do it. We had never done these things before, but we achieved them. We were pumped up and sent off. Sometimes we glanced back for assurance; our families and teachers were there and we knew they expected us to do it. We did. We succeeded. We achieved. We continued the confident march as they expected.

On many of these expeditions we didn't march alone. There were others building expectations with us—training, we called it. Sometimes we didn't even glance back, we were so confident of our companions' support.

Most of these were minor expectations—going on the bus by ourselves, or going to the store alone. But some were great expectations—completing twelve to sixteen years of school and earning a diploma. We developed morals. We developed responsibility.

Then we got another lift. We started work, and our supervisor boosted us with more expectations. They were almost as basic to work as our parents' expectations were to growing up. They were part of the continuing growth to maturity.

Then the problem started: "Grow up, bunkie! School's over! You're on your own now."

The stream of expectations created for us by others slowed down, and it happened at the same time that our other adult responsibilities were growing. "Oh, we forgot to tell you, but you must design most of your own expectations from now on." Don't panic. Salvation lies in the two great themes of expectation. They offer you hope beyond all reason:

> You will act as you are expected to act.
> You will achieve what you are expected to achieve.
>
> You will act as you expect to act.
> You will achieve what you expect to achieve.

Both are true. Both are inherently accepted. Neither often challenged. They are never fully understood, much like fundamental forces of nature.

Expectation is personal confidence that you will make something happen. It's not just hope. Hope is only a desire, a wish that it will happen, sometimes just a dream. But when you add commitment to your hope, you've gone a long way toward making that hope a personal expectation. Commitment is like a trigger inside; when it flips, you know you've converted to expectation.

I know that all hopes don't have to become expectations to succeed. Many of the great and humble reach for and achieve many things for which they have only the faintest of hope. Certainly it's a tougher fight, and a more satisfying victory, to achieve without expectation. But that's one of my persistent points: In your career game, creating expectation, and winning with expectation, is far easier than you now realize. All of your scores will surprise you.

THE GREAT THEMES OF EXPECTATION

Most of us have experienced the thrill of fulfilling personal expectations. We also watch similar successes being made by friends and associates. An experience of this kind often provides a new insight into someone whose strength and quality we didn't previously appreciate. We realize sometimes that these demonstrations of growth and strength are equally surprising to the person, a new insight to himself or herself.

But few of us organize our observations and understandings into useful, systematic tools to use expectation deliberately. The published themes of expectation can become valuable aids to our personal experiences and observations. They compress time and isolate the elements of particular situations. Our own experiences often obscure the real issues and opportunities because they're spread over long periods of time filled with many concurrent events. The great published themes—predigest, shape, and communicate—are the concepts and solutions available as working tools. They also motivate us to encourage deliberate experiments, either as a game or as dedicated efforts for personal growth.

You will expand and stimulate your use of the concepts of expectation when you read these three great themes of expectation. The best-known modern theme of expectation is the play *Pygmalion*, by George Bernard Shaw. An article derived partly from the play, "Pygmalion in Management," by J. Sterling Livingston, was published in the *Harvard Business Review*, July–August 1969. (The original Greek myth, *Pygmalion*, is more general but still worth searching for and reading.) The musical version, *My Fair Lady*, is the best-known today. In it, Professor Henry Higgins makes a bet that he can transform Eliza Doolittle, a flower girl from the streets of London, and pass her off as a lady.

There are two great themes in *Pygmalion*. Many people only remember the first and most obvious: Professor Higgins does transform Eliza from flower girl to lady. He changes her speech first, and then her manner, to that of a duchess. She becomes like a puppet to his will. By the efforts of Professor Higgins, by his ideas and his persistence, a new Eliza is created.

But even as the transformation is progressing, we sense the fires of another change building in Eliza. A second miracle, even greater, is taking place: The puppet is cutting the strings that bind her to her creator. Eliza's new image of herself no longer lets her accept others' treatment of her as a flower girl. She says, in effect: "I am free. I expect certain treatment from you." This new Eliza, this lady, then proceeds to exercise her newly realized power. She has some surprise and confusion, but she moves out to fulfill her freedom, to be responsible for herself in her new world. She can never be a puppet again. And even Professor Higgins is astonished at this free creature who has grown from his experiment.

The potential for that kind of transformation lies within you, within us all. Whether it is called forth by my words, or someone else's, depends on you. My concern is for all of those who never hear the call.

Eliza's transformation is no more dramatic than real-life transformations that you will see when you open your eyes to these personal changes in people. Perhaps you have had equally dramatic personal changes. Again, many of these changes within yourself and others are obscured by time stretches and other events until you search for them.

Conscious recognition of them didn't come to me suddenly. For many years I simply didn't realize that one person could make such changes in another. When the dawning came, I remember reviewing several cases and recognizing that they were perfect fits to the concepts of expectation.

When I was beginning to understand expectation, an actual case dramatized it for me. The incident was modest; I mentioned in Chapter 2 the blossoming of a young woman who seemed to me to have the poorest of potential. I couldn't believe her very capable supervisor had brought in such poor material. Yet the supervisor never had any doubt; the supervisor had true expectation.

She proceeded to transform that young woman to a person of recognized competence, a person of independence.

The second miracle—self-transformation—is one of the master patterns of success waiting, begging, to be used by you to create your personal growth. You can develop and use that process again and again.

Now bring the two great expectations into balance. Your supervisor's expectations for you can shape and inspire your motivation to bring a revolution to your personal growth and career. You need this contribution to your development. Am I saying or implying that your career is dependent on your supervisor's expectations of you? If he or she expects great things, will you achieve great things? If he or she expects failure, will you fail?

I say it can be that way, *but only if you let it*. Have no doubt that the boost of your supervisor is a key determinant of your career. You need that boost, but in most cases you are the major determinant of the expectation that your supervisor has for you; you have power and opportunity unlimited to shape his or her expectations. This is a company loop, continually producing the expectations for you, your supervisor, yourself, and your work group.

Create in your supervisor expectations for you that he or she doesn't have presently. Create in yourself expectations that you don't have presently.

Getting to your supervisor is that upward stream of experience again. There are several ways of doing it. Some are outright manipulation and exploitation. The prime one is simple excellence in work. Use both, but use manipulation ethically.

Your supervisor's game is work. He or she is the first tier of management. The company relies on supervisors to get its work done.

When you work well, and particularly when you create improved ways of working, you get your supervisor's attention. When you do these recurrently, you create expectation in your supervisor for you. This is your one best way.

But your supervisor's expectations can never replace your need to create your own expectations for yourself. That is an essential part of your freedom and maturity. "Fine," you say, "but either you have it or you don't. Life's like that." Not so. You can grow from your own expectations.

EXPERIMENTING WITH EXPECTATION

You can experiment with your expectation as easily as you can experiment with seeds and plants in a greenhouse. You can grow your own expectations like you grow flowers. You can experiment with your own expectations of yourself. You can experiment with shaping your supervisor's expectations of you. You can play it as a game completely without risk, or you can play it as a game for high stakes.

Regardless of the stakes you choose, the play is the same: You decide to do it and you commit to do something by a particular date. If you recall some of your past ideas, choose one and start. If you don't have a good one now, start by committing to define one by your target date. Make the first one small. Expectation is knowing that you will do it. You will succeed. Then do it again, something a little bigger, but not too soon.

Try both kinds: first, just your own expectation; then try shaping your supervisor's expectations. The latter is a longer project; do it in parallel with other games. Remember, the one obvious opportunity for this is your performance review procedure. Whether or not you are asked for your plans for the coming period, make some. Keep them simple at first, things that you know you will achieve. Follow up, confirm that you are keeping your expectations alive, doing what you say you will do. If you play for high stakes, you will miss a few. Don't worry about the misses if it is clear that your wins were well worth the effort.

PYGMALION IN MANAGEMENT

The concepts of Livingston's great article have influenced me for years. He uses superb illustrations and explanations of the power of expectations between supervisors and subordinates. He reaches further by showing self-created reactions of people who realize that expectations for them are lower than for others, lower than they are willing to accept.

Livingston's emphasis is different from mine. I want you to understand the power of expectation between people, which is his key point. More than that, I want you to recognize and use the expectation that you can create within yourself. To paraphrase Livingston's statement: By *your* effort and *your* will, you can transform yourself.

HOW ONE MAN USED EXPECTATION

I opened this chapter by describing the good fortune of initiating my career by entering a group headed by a person of high expectation. I will close it by describing a person for whom a vaulting expectation had just been born. Both of these cases had a major effect on my life. During both, I was conscious of the major change, but I did not recognize the patterns, or how to use them, until several years later. A part of my realization of how success systems operate was to look back and understand the games that were played by now-successful people. How did they succeed?

What failed, and why? What were the patterns as they moved from average to successful?

When I met this man, I think his great personal potential had just dawned on him. I think he recognized that several powerful forces (and luck) were working together.

His new assignment was a breakthrough. He had succeeded at his previous assignment, a step up and a real test. In that one, he, a man with a weak high school education, had supervised people with backgrounds similar to his own. Now nearly all of his people were college graduates. But since his new assignment included planning for his previous operation and several similar operations, he already knew where the opportunities for growth and improvement were, and how to make the changes.

This man had been tagged with the expectation of mediocrity, both by himself and by others, as an extension of his educational background.

His background, a contrast of weak credentials and strong performance, and his new understanding of latent greatness, must have been his insight when I met him. Our company was not just tolerant of ambition; we were excited with shared needs, shared goals, and shared growth. We were forging a new kind of company, and we knew it. We were led by managers with a vision, people who would use all the employees would make available. The managers were intolerant of credentials that didn't produce, but their reaction was how to *induce* contribution—or seduce, if necessary.

This person seemed to sense the convergence of all of these things and his part in it. He understood what needed to be done; the urgent schedule was clear to him; he had resources, not as many experienced people as he needed, but a complement of enthusiastic, motivated people of potential. Along with these, the door to great potential wealth had opened a crack.

But I think the big blockbuster that overlaid it all was the dual vision of expectation that he had. It wasn't hope; it was the realization that he could do it, that we could do it. You see, both of the themes in *Pygmalion* were not only pervasive in him, he understood both of them: He recognized what the expectations of his managers had done for him, but he was also free. He knew now that he could create the same kinds of expectations for himself. He understood his obligation to project his expectations to us, individually and as a group.

This was a different environment from the first one that I described. My early one was a challenge, charged with change in a great, mature company. This later one was a tough situation, working for a tough, ambitious man. It was high opportunity, but also high in risk; when you made a mistake, you heard about it in no uncertain terms. We worked sixty-hour weeks, and sometimes more, with no pay for overtime. But some things were the same. We knew we were good; we had expectations; we knew we'd lose a few, and blood flowed when we did. And in front of us marched this man with the new expectation, his new realization that he could perform as a real manager in a well-managed company. With him, we knew and practiced the simple disciplines that are the basis of work: we set goals; we made plans; we controlled.

I don't propose for you a grand scheme by which you change your whole person—as this man did—with no assured route to becoming a captain of industry. I do ask you to confirm my words and concepts by personal observation and analysis of the great achievements of others, to realize that they started with the same potential that you have, and then to make your decision and design your own success.

6

Career Goals

Some authorities advise you to take stock of yourself and your situation before you set your career goals. They say this will keep you from setting unrealistic goals and risking disappointment.

Don't do this! Don't take stock of yourself first. Don't even be afraid to risk disappointment. Your present evaluation of your abilities, capacities, and potential is only a fraction of your true value. Before setting your goals, look instead at the great achievements of people you respect.

Many of these people were once in the same starting position you're in. Somehow they learned, they realized what the game is; somehow, the dawning came. How you use yourself is more important than what you are when you start. The stature of people you respect, any greatness they have now, grew as they proceeded on the career path to their goals. It was probably not there when they started.

Concentrate on two things as you set your first tentative goals. Look at the achievements and positions of others, including the personal price they paid. Then locate yourself relative to these good performers; what work, what achievements, do you think offer satisfaction to you? Then choose where you want to be five years from now.

Now test your goal. Can you sketch a series of milestones connecting your present situation with your tentative goal?

A primary career milestone is a combination of a job and a time. "I intend to be a line supervisor in June, two years from now," or "I intend to be a personnel counselor in October, three years from now." If you haven't changed jobs recently, you need a job milestone within twelve months. In this period, you should have a significant promotion or a lateral job change.

In any case, the acid test of your tentative goal is the validity of the near-term actions that you must take to start on the path. Can you define the immediate achievements that you expect to make to reach your first milestone? If you can't, go back and reconsider your goal.

This kind of goal adjustment is not a one-way street. When you test your milestones and rough plans, you can raise your goal; either set a shorter schedule or reach for greater growth in the same time period. If your near milestones are clear, don't worry that your distant ones are hazy. You can clarify them as you get closer.

Here's an illustration that's literally corny. I'm no farmer, but I've been told that this is the way to plow a straight furrow, and I can testify that it works when I cut my grass: Fix your eye on a distant point and start toward it. As you push, glance down to dodge the nearby obstacles. Then get back on the track and keep pushing

but the initiative had to come from her. She and I talked of our jobs and their content. We explored her personal experience and her background in school. She became interested and took steps to move into effective work.

This kind of discussion should always lead the inquirer to consider work where she or he has had no previous experience or interest. For instance, many women still don't realize that they can learn drafting, operate precision machinery, and perform other jobs traditionally held by men.

Another factor to consider in identifying jobs is the ongoing evolution to simplify work. This complements your own career growth: You're going up the ladder in capability, and the jobs are coming down to meet you in lowered requirements. Jobs are simplified through experience and learning, better machinery, and improvements in information processing. This provides an opportunity for you to step up: You can identify likely jobs and ask for one as a challenge; you can demonstrate that the job you choose is ready for challenged lower-level people.

All of this indicates that both jobs and people are in transition. Your career goals are jobs that represent growth for you. Your plan must recognize how the jobs will become available. If the job exists, you must plan on an incumbent moving out. If you think the job will be created by an organization change, you have a chancy situation. You may have to design your job and cause it to happen. Often this is easier than you might think. Before you design your own, consider what you can do with a little luck.

POP-UP TARGETS

Working to develop career goals opens your eyes to opportunities that you don't recognize otherwise. I've seen this happen frequently. It is akin to the next-opening-is-yours custom.

While developing goals, you may spot just the job that attracts you. Here is an actual case.

A man in his late thirties wanted a job change. He had no complaint about pay, but he was concerned that his career growth showed signs of slowing. He had spoken to his boss about a year previously. His boss was receptive, but nothing came from the discussion. He spoke to the boss's boss six months later. Again, he was well received, but with no results. I asked him what particular job or what kind of job he wanted. He didn't know—just a change.

How could he expect someone to develop a future for him? It happens, but it is asking for a haphazard career.

We discussed the goal-setting method and schedule. He was enthusiastic. He returned after two weeks with the vague "I want to be a manager" routine. Realizing that this wouldn't pass my test for a career goal, he went back to the drawing board to come up with a good one—on the six-week schedule.

Three weeks later I saw him in the hall. His face lit up and I greeted him with, "Well, I see you already have the new job that you wanted." He looked surprised and wanted to know who told me. I explained that I knew from his expression and the fact that it frequently happens that when you're on the lookout for opportunity, you actually create it from the events of your day.

Here's what had happened. While he was in a meeting, someone discussed a major vendor problem. The speaker dropped a casual remark that we should consider manufacturing a problem product. That was enough for this man. In a few days he developed a proposal, thought it over a day or so, and presented it to his supervisor. Things moved fast and he was assigned to manage the project. It was just what he needed. He was in the goal-seeking mode and a casual remark lit his fuse.

DESIGNING A NEW JOB

You may have to design your own job to get into the work or organization that you want. Assume that you want to make a fairly radical change in your career path. Initially, you may need an interim job that combines your present experience with the new work that you want.

To use a specific example, assume you have worked in manufacturing and control, but you want to move into the field of computers and data processing. What kind of approach can you use? Ask, "What do I have that they need?" Computer people are persistently short on experience and understanding of operations, but these are just what you're long on. This makes you a natural to work in some of the interfaces between data processing and the operating people they serve.

You can start by working with computer people who are in contact with operating people. Computer people can use you as a realistic substitute for contact with operations. Alternatively, you can become an active interface; with a brief computer background, you can be accepted as the computer people's representative. At the same time, operations people will feel that they finally have someone inside who represents them and understands their problems. This new job becomes an interim goal for you.

GOALS THAT AREN'T GOALS

Earlier in this chapter I described two common bum starts in setting career goals—long-term stretch goals. I mentioned that when you set such goals, you can test them by trying to fit milestones into the gap between the present and the goal that is three to five years, or more, in the future. These fill-in milestones are necessary to reach the goals; if they fit well, your goals are probably good.

Similarly, the action steps required in the months and weeks immediately ahead can be used to test your goals. If all seem achievable, even if unfamiliar or tough, you probably have a good set of goals.

These near-term actions are somewhat different from the longer-term major career goals. They are smaller, more specific tasks that you must accomplish now. They are the actions that require discussion with your supervisor. He or she is probably more concerned with them than with your long-term personal goals. After all, these are the essence of the shared goals, the things you and your supervisor have to do together now.

These near-term goals suffer more from vagueness than the two bum starts of the long-term goals. I've heard and read a lot of poor ones, including some of my own. Here are some examples of such near-term goals that aren't goals:

Continue to sustain and improve my contribution

Make efforts to do so-and-so

Assist in getting better organized

Make better use of the clerks and secretaries

Consider returning to school for my degree

Increase my understanding of our objectives

See if I can improve our file organization

Look at suggested changes with a positive attitude

Generally, these are vague, lack commitment, and need dates for measurement. "Continue to sustain and improve" is just fluff. "Make efforts" says I may try something but don't care to be measured.

Take "better organized" and "better use of clerks" and combine them to make something good: "We have five accountants and three clerks presently working on the general ledger, a five-to-three ratio. I propose to reorganize, revise jobs, and make major cost savings. We should be able to do a better job with two accountants and five clerks. I have a seven-month plan to make this change."

"Consider returning to school" is more fluff. Remember, even done right, it's a resource goal worth only 10 percent of a work goal. Try "I will return to school in September for education in support of XYZ work goal."

A little fluff at the end may be worthwhile. If you have several good, defined, measurable work goals, some unmeasurable commitments to improve your personal style can enlist needed help from your supervisor. An example is your intention to express appreciation more routinely and promptly for work well done. Your boss can help you in improving this kind of habit.

COMBINED GOALS—WORK AND PAY

Develop your pay goals along with your work goals. Satisfying work is related to your pay in ways far more complex than we can understand. We can generalize about how age-old societies rewarded poets versus hunters, but I doubt that any of us truly understands our need and drive for pay.

Dedicate a little time and work to learn the basics of the pay game, your company's in particular. You may want to skim the section on pay, Chapters 10 through 12, now. I will illustrate the combined development of goals for work and pay with an example parallel to the pay goals illustrated in these later chapters.

If your goal is to advance in your present field, you can usually see several years further into your future. Assume that you are an engineer and intend to stay in engineering; this makes it fairly easy to look ahead four to eight years to set combined work and pay goals. If instead of staying in engineering you intend to transfer to marketing, it may be harder to plan more than three to five years.

Present Job and Pay

"I am a junior engineer. My present pay is about 5 percent below the midpoint of pay for my job and job grade. It is about 75 pecent of the top pay for my job."

That is the right way to think of your present pay situation. First, think where you are in the scale—where your present pay is relative to the midpoint. "I can go this much farther in the pay bracket for this job." Without considering actual pay dollars, this locates you on the pay map at any time. Even continuing inflation won't confuse the picture when you describe it this way. Your position is defined and your progress is measurable.

How do you get this kind of information? In some companies it is posted or published; in others, you have to dig for it. If it's not readily available, that's a clue that "they" may not want you to know, so proceed cautiously. If you have some of the key information, you can combine it with what you learn from the chapters on pay and build the complete pay map of your company.

Next, where are you going?

Engineering Supervisor—Eight Years

You set a tentative goal to be an engineering supervisor eight years from now. Assume that the pay schedules of your company are published or that you have broken the code. There are clues galore supporting whether your goal is feasible and how much it pays. You look at people presently in the job. You see their cars, homes, and furnishings. You know their intelligence and capability. You know their motivation and how long they have worked. Now you compare your present situation with what their situation was eight years ago. You can do it! Your goal is a good one! In fact, you may even do a little better.

Get more specific on the pay goal. If the job map is available, you know that you must move through the Engineer and Senior Engineer jobs to get to Engineering Supervisor. That means a job promoton every two to three years. If you have only clues and not facts, you can guess that the pay for the Engineering Supervisor job is nearly double that of your present job. (This may seem exaggerated, but my experience shows that we all initially underestimate the size of the pay steps; remember that the pay steps must be big enough to get to the supervisor's pay with only a few levels in between.)

If you aim for the middle of the pay range for the Engineering Supervisor in eight years, you will nearly double your real pay. Any increases to the pay structure during that time will be stacked on top of that, but probably won't buy anything. What's important is that you define jobs and positions in the pay ranges that fit your time schedule. You won't be very accurate. You'll beat your schedule in the better years and lose a little in the poor ones. Regardless of inflation, you will know where you are on the track that you laid out. Chances are good that you will change direction and also step up the pace if you manage well.

These goals involve a major reach. The following story illustrates how only a major reach will get you out of the little-bit-better-tomorrow mode. This is an example of major goals at work; it started with company goals, but they were company goals only because they were shared by the people involved.

Some years ago my company was striving to grow to a $25 million company. We pushed hard—late nights, Saturdays, all of it. We did it! We broke the $2 million-a-month mark. We gathered for a meeting, expecting congratulatons and accolades from the chief. His recognition of our triumph was sincere but brief—he expected it, he knew we could do it, but he had more important things to talk about.

He dropped the bomb: Our new goal was $250 million a year—ten times growth in ten years! We were stunned, but when we left, we truly understood; we shared his goal, his expectation. Walking out, we were already figuring how to reach it, building our part of the new model, our share.

Only he seemed to understand how good we were, how much we could achieve, collectively and individually. Only this kind of major reach will get you out of the little-bit-better-tomorrow mode.

COMPETITION

I have described the career game with little or no attention to career competition or company politics. For the most part I ignore them in discussions, just as I ignore them in work. Concentrating on the work has been my solution.

My experience, both personal and with coworkers, is that in a good company competition is not a significant career factor in the middle or lower ranks. If you choose to knock on the executive door, you have moved to a league different from the game I know.

I encounter people who view their companies, including my own, as closed and cliquish. I cannot say they are wrong, only that when I have worked in the same company, these factors did not affect me, or were not there. Most of the time I see the company's opportunities as being completely available, and exploitable, to the person who manages his or her career. Accordingly, that opportunity occupies most of my discussion.

GOAL INTERPLAY

Since a company is people working together toward shared goals, there is tremendous opportunity for interplay between personal and company goals. The following case illustrates major interaction between personal and company goals. It involved a major project, full of opportunity and risk for hundreds of people, a situation where all of these people, and our company, had to work out new goals. Such a project, very large and extremely risky, affected hundreds of people and involved millions of dollars and many vendors over several years. This was the rare breakthrough opportunity. It was a notch below the you-bet-your-career situation.

The goals of the project were the goals of its leader. Some of the goals had been modified from above, or out of deference to a major team member. If achieved, they would affect a significant part of future company life. The project represented a radical displacement of a large, embedded group of operating people, thus exploding into a truly vital mainstream operations game.

Our success depended on a technical peformance which had never been demonstrated. If we succeeded, we would leapfrog a whole generation of evolution. If we failed we would continue on the slow, evolutionary path.

All of the people associated with the old ways and the new project had career goal decisions to make. From the first rumor, they had several years of self-questioning: "Do I join the innovators, or do I stick with the old? Will it work? Will they have me if I ask?" And later, "Did I make the right decision?" These questions and a hundred others persisted and recurred for the life of the project.

Career goal decisions in this situation were different from the self-centered kind that represent elective goal decisions. If people weren't associated with the project, joining was their elective decision, but their schedules weren't elective. Their entry could be limited or controlled by what phase the project was in. Their entry opportunities could be gone in a month. If they were in the old guard, they had to join immediately or risk being displaced a year later. And joining later could mean that the choice jobs would be gone by that time. Whether inside the project or outside in the affected area, everyone was aware of the effect on his or her personal goals. People who had never expressed personal goals before became aware that they had latent, unexpressed goals. Now they were forced to take a position.

Goals and risks became frequently associated subjects of discussion because in a project like this, the risks were as relatively large as the potential prize. (In elective goal situations, risk can be controlled by you.)

The goals of the project manager and his inner circle were particularly interesting. The visionaries had no thought of failure. The prophets of doom, like moths and the flame, tended to measure people on the short side. The chief listened to all sides, but leaned to the front—he expected and got many successes and a few failures.

CONCLUSION

Your goals change with your progress, your failures, and your assessment of new experiences. People clash and influence each other. Assignments change with personal and company phases, with successes, and with failures.

You will see both types of career goals—those which you generate and control yourself, and those that arise when you join a group

CONCLUSION   99

project and are therefore largely designed for you. The by-invitation type may not arise from a large project such as I have described, but many of its variables may be set already when you volunteer or are invited to join the group. I've seen a few that seem preset for failure, but they are rare. In a good company, there are always good ones available.

7

Your Game

The fun part of your game starts when you have some goals. Your goals may change later, but for now you're planning, plotting, and scheming to make them happen. You're weaving into your daily work these small additional moves and actions that mean a different career tomorrow. Those changes are the essence of this book.

In playing your career game, keep a proper perspective on it and on your company's game. The changes that I ask you to make are only a small proportion of your work; they vitalize your career like seasoning enhances food. Your work is still 95 percent mainstream work, the lifeblood of your company. Getting your changes going takes some time; you're not going to walk in tomorrow and work in a higher level and get paid a dollar more.

The new threads that you need to weave into the fabric of your work are the continuing threads of career growth and direction.

But the base fabric of your career is still day-to-day work, the stream of production, the basic stuff of your job. And remember that the game approach—personal or company—does not imply a lighter task. It's a way of making work more satisfying, more valuable.

Your career is a forty-year game. Some play it longer, some retire earlier. There are two basic ways to play and two basic ways to finish. Some people, even early in the game, can't wait for it to be over, to withdraw. Others, who play it with relish and satisfaction, leave it reluctantly. Playing with the second group is a lot more fun.

During your forty years, you will have five to fifteen jobs, either changes in levels of work or assignments in different fields of work. If you assume a role in controlling your changes, your chances for fun, satisfaction, and growth—and more pay—are a lot greater. *My* game is to get you to try.

Three kinds of actions make up your personal game. First are your actions that I call personal *style*, your common daily personal habits of work and interaction with people in your company. Second, your *tactics* are the little plans, plots, and schemes—either one-shot actions or ones that you use repeatedly, with or without adaptations—that you use on the problem at hand. Tactics are the most fun of the career game. Third, *strategies* are the bedrock, least changeable, and stabilizing activities of your career.

None of these kinds of personal actions is new to you. You may not have thought of them in this way, but you already practice them. They are not clearly separate from each other, and they interact as you play your game. I'll discuss tactics first because they are more fun and make up the most active part of career management.

TACTICS—PLAYS, SCHEMES, AND PLOTS

Career tactics are your action plans for the near months, to change the way you work. A set of good tactics in support of your goal, with a schedule, is the model of your career plan. Is it a plan? No, one thing is missing. Until you overlay your career model with *commitment*—the expectation of making it happen—it's only the shell of a plan.

I want you to have a plan even if you only operate it from time to time. At the very least, develop and use a few tactics now and later. If you do, you'll be hooked. You can succeed with tactics alone—not as much or as consistently as if you had a real career plan—but you will succeed.

We have already discussed several tactics: Working Around the Boss, the One-Shot-Resignation-Feint, and the Performance Review Initiative. Tactics are like good jokes; you hear a lot and recognize a million, but you only remember a few. I use three typical ones when I speak before an audience. I like them because someone always smiles in recognition when I mention their names: "October Triumph," "Underground Projects," and "One-Eyed Kings." Before I discuss each of these, I want to briefly mention some others.

"Get Inside First" is a tactic of personal mobility. If you want to work in a particular company or organization, take any reasonable job to enter the organization. Once inside, move yourself to the assignment and level of work that you want. The same approach applies to converting to a new field of work; take any reasonable assignment to acquire the job title, recognition, and experience in the new field.

Some tactics that are commonly recognized are either misunderstood or are actually wrong: "Train Your Replacement" is one of these. It is hard to deny that it is good to have someone in your organization trained to take over in your absence, or to cover critical work for short periods. A supervisor who encourages people to train for this usually has plenty of people who want to enter his or her organization.

But this tactic can go too far. The same person who fills in for every absence is regarded as "tagged for takeover." He or she is the heir-apparent. Other qualified candidates may become discouraged and leave. Underlings may court the anointed one; discipline suffers. To top it off, many of the designated successors may fail.

A much better tactic to prepare for your promotion and the changing of the guard is to pass the crown around. When possible, the high mogul randomly assigns all who have minimum qualifications to act in his or her absence, each time with the expectation that the designated person will do the job well.

"Forcing Yes" is a cross between a tactic and a personal style. When you need something, make your request specific and direct while maintaining steady eye contact. It's hard for most people to say no to you under these conditions. You have a high probability of getting a yes.

Many of us are poor at handling these kinds of requests in spontaneous conversation. Don't worry. Lay your plan and organize your conversation beforehand. Explore alternate turns the conversation may take and reactions you might use. Resolve to speak slowly. Don't get excited or angry. Resolve not to end with a postponed decision.

"I WANT This Job" is a version of the same tactic. When you have decided on a job you want, let someone know who will be involved in filling it. Be careful how you indicate your interest. Don't say you'd "like to be considered." Say "I WANT the job." Leave no doubt that you really want the job, but respect the incumbent and your responsibility to your present supervisor.

Regardless of which tactic you use, there are some common ground rules: Limit carefully the people with whom you discuss your plans. Don't babble about your game. This is especially true of the multiple dreams that pass through your head; everyone has them but if you discuss all of them, people regard you as undedicated or unstable.

You owe extra consideration to your supervisor. Let him or her know first when you can. After all, you may work together again (or vice versa).

October Triumphs

October Triumphs is a general tactic of timing. For some career actions, success is completely determined by timing. Originally, October was a sly reference to the schedule of the performance review in my company and many other companies.

Everyone involved in performance reviews is cautioned to give proper weight to people's performance during the whole period of the review. This is a near-impossible task for most. We have all heard jokes based on "What have you done for me lately?" No matter how hard we try, we give more weight to the most recent events of performance.

If you can, schedule your tactics to culminate when they yield the greatest effect—when the review is being made and the rewards determined. Have no twinges of conscience about this; it also means that your company will expect more from you in the future—next October.

are people of solid success, whose support is essential to the victories of the leader. Their shares of the success have been great. Some of these people are noticeably lopsided but, in combination and with leadership, have fused into great teams. Interestingly, some of the most lopsided never recognize the fact and strike out for personal triumph that never comes.

Deciding simply to take things as they come, with no goals and no plan, can still bring you exceptional success if you use the chance opportunities well and perk up your tactics and style a bit.

But assuming that you elect the strategy of deliberate career management, what next? You must consider several more strategies. The direction of your career path is a good one to consider next. Then tackle a possible strategy of personal growth and renewal.

VERTICAL OR LATERAL MOVES?

Are you so determined to remain an accountant or an engineer that you don't want to consider lateral job movements? That may be a good decision for you now. It can be changed later if you wish, but many people start with the intention of getting experience and perspective from the viewpoints of several different jobs. In Chapter 6 I described the engineer who intends to stay in engineering. Generally, moving is easier earlier in your career. Getting the opportunity is easier and there is less personal disruption. You can learn many of the basics equally well in any assignment that you choose. If you are in a technical field or other rapidly evolving specialty, you may have to maintain an active parallel effort to keep sharp in your field.

Whether you choose vertical growth or multiple lateral moves, develop a sense of the strategies of your company and industry. In the broad sense, all business is concerned with "Create, Make, Market, and Support" activities; this is a good framework for thinking of strategies. (There are only a few strategies, goals, and policies associated with each of these major activities. Being aware of them is interesting, easy, and can be valuable.)

There is a point in personal growth where strategic awareness is not optional. I have known people who were unaware that their narrow interests were limiting their growth. Doing your homework by reading, and extending that knowledge with company contacts, is an effective tactic for personal growth.

THE CHOSEN

Among the people who don't need strategies and plans are "The Chosen." These are the few whose tactics and styles are dominated by simple, continued excellence.

Their success seems to result from two common characteristics: early commitment to their company and their work, and personal acceptance that they will pay a high price. Their pattern of success is: work, learn, and ask for more. Their careers seem to be characterized by a period of stage setting of six to eight years.

They make mistakes, but their mistakes are concealed by their prodigious output, double to triple the average. With some exceptions, these people are noncreative but they are extra-sensitive to the need for continual innovation. Often they have a blind spot (the fact that they are not creative). They think they are innovative. They actively encourage and support innovation.

Many of the chosen seem not to have strong personal goals as such. Once they have satisfied themselves that the goals of the company are good, they accept these as their personal goals. The part of the company goal assigned them at the moment is their personal goal of the moment. Continual success on these assigned goals is their personal success.

Are these special people, or can you join them? Both.

Some of them seem to have no choice; they appear to be chosen before they join a company. Many seem to receive the spark much later, inspired by a teacher or a supervisor, or unwilling to accept mediocrity that they observe in others early in their career. Their only decision seems to be whether to answer the call. Their stage setting seems to be a period of searching for the patterns—the patterns of the company, the patterns of successful careers, and the success patterns of successful people in their company.

About the eighth year they truly seem to be chosen. They are called for a significant assignment. The expectation for their success is pervasive—it's shared by their own supervisor, the management team, peers, and all. Other assignments follow this success. The attachment between company and person grows closer, appears to satisfy a joint need. The strategies and styles of person and company appear to be the same. Once chosen, it is difficult to tell whether these people are pulling the company along or the company is pulling them.

There are few of these people. Even among the group recognized as the most successful in a company, they are only a fraction. This may be your game.

STRATEGY FOR PERSONAL GROWTH AND RENEWAL

This phrase sounds so grand, complex, and intellectual that I'm reluctant to use it. Actually, a personal strategy for growth and renewal is simple and requires few decisions. Do you recognize the need for it, and are you going to do it? One answer only.

If yes, your actions for your early career—the first ten years—will be similar, regardless of your path. You must soak up the experience and knowledge of work; you must keep up by reading in your field; and you probably need more formal education or an intense equivalent.

Your mature career—the last half of your working life—is tougher. If you've achieved the higher levels in your company, the work tends to induce growth and renewal. Answer the call of work, and you will continue to grow with developments.

For the rest of us who travel paths of low-level careers—and that's most of us—it is a dangerous path skirting the edge of a cliff. On our right is the pit of personal obsolescence; the bears in the pit consume those who fall behind or lose their enthusiasm.

I really believe it's a use-it-or-lose-it proposition. If you don't keep a lively interest in your work, you've got a problem at any age. You must take action at least to replace your obsolete capabilities or you will fall behind. There are trade-offs involved: in your maturity some of your experience can be substituted for a little less energy or knowledge of the latest techniques. But don't expect to be enthroned as a guru—there isn't a need for many.

YOUR OWN STYLE

Your own style has to do with "presence," the mysterious relationship between people. This is a powerful personal strength which you can develop and never stop developing.

For instance, you recognize that you have been captured by someone's presence when you realize that an actor has transported you to another world for a moment. You have radiated presence when the maitre d' tags you as a child of the rich, which you aren't.

I use the word "presence" sincerely. You can develop presence so that when you ask for the keys to the kingdom the keeper's only response is, "The gold or the platinum?" When you ask for the innermost secrets of the company with presence, you get more than you need. When you ask an unknown fellow employee for assistance, with presence, you find you have to caution him or her, that yours is a minor need: "Don't shut down your whole operation to help me." All of these things say that your presence – your style – earns you the trust of other people. They will help you; they will give you access to information.

Presence is a transmission of expectation from you to someone from whom you need cooperation. It is a combination of lateral power and motivation. Good people at all levels like you to ask for their help; asking brings forth responsive grace. Oddly enough, this kind of giving seems to accept no thanks or repayment. The sole compensation seems to be the act of giving itself. One twist is important: When you use the results of such giving, reserve crediting your source until you're absolutely certain that your use reflects to his credit.

Over the years, in several companies, I have experienced assistance from people who gave to me in this way. I know that this element of personal style will become a tremendous help to you.

YOUR GAME WON'T WORK IN MY COMPANY

"It might work in some companies, but it won't work in my company." In most cases, the few people who make this remark are referring to the excellent pay raises you can earn by managing your career in a good company. This game works in any good company – not necessarily outstanding, not even excellent, just a *good* company. If your company is at least good, some good people have to be earning average annual raises of 15 percent for at least fifteen initial years of career growth.

Although I will discuss the game of pay and raises very specifically in Chapters 10 through 12, I want to preview it here because the pay opportunity is so much a part of the motivation for your career game.

The "it won't work" comment always comes from people who haven't played the game; it nearly always comes from people who never play the game. They always cite that "raises and pay are tightly budgeted in my company."

But that's just the opportunity you want! "Tightly budgeted" is synonymous with good practice, and good practice means opportunity. If you perform well above average, you will be rewarded well above average in new work opportunities, and in pay.

"Tightly budgeted" spells double opportunity. Raises are budgeted based on averages. No matter how much is budgeted for average, excellent gets twice that amount, and minimum gets half that amount. That's a four-to-one range from excellent to minimum. If average is 10 percent, the high is 20 percent and the low is 5 percent. That's a great opportunity range.

There's more. No structured budget is made without pads for contingencies. Each layer of management above your supervisor has a contingency raise budget to award outstanding people; this is the "unadvertised special," and you can be special one or two years out of three. For pay, the company's game provides the opportunity; my game is for you to use the opportunity.

No company's game is exactly like this. Yours may not even be structured with a procedure. It doesn't matter. If it's a good, informal system, you can use it the same way; perform and you'll get the good raises.

How do you get your share of this kind of opportunity, this kind of pay? How do you play this kind of game?

First, you study and understand the people and the rules of your company. Next, you make minor safe plays to confirm that you understand, to build your confidence, and to get comfortable with the game. Then you're ready to escalate and play the full game. Don't listen for the glory of drums rolling and trumpets blowing because your full game may be a very modest one.

Some of this "how" is easy to describe and illustrate, and easy to do. But much of it involves your personal style, your supervisor's and your company's. You must develop your personal style yourself. It may or may not be easy for you.

The rules of your company's game are little different from those of Checkers or other games, but many of them are not written. Get whatever is written and read it; your time won't be wasted. The unwritten information you need is a mixture of DOs and DON'Ts applicable to any company.

THE DON'Ts

A general Don't derives from this truth: You can't bargain for pay with your supervisor. Don't try; you would just create an uncomfortable situation between you and your supervisor, or between your supervisor and those above. People who don't understand this concept ask for a firm commitment on their next pay raise or promotion. Common questions they ask are, "What do I have to do for you to raise me to job grade 8 next time?" or "If I do so-and-so, will you raise my pay a given amount?"

No supervisor can commit to such requests. However, most of them bear the scars of having tried to do so early in their careers. They have learned that many things intervene and prevent them from fullfilling commitments: the person's performance declines, but he or she won't admit it; another person's performance rises unexpectedly; a superior person transfers in; an economic decline prevents promotions and good raises—the list is endless.

An ultimatum is even worse than the impossible bargain. In a good company, nearly any ultimatum is taken as an offer to resign. I remember a manager making a controversial proposal and winding up with, "I don't care to continue this assignment with any other approach." The man thought he was negotiating. His boss didn't; he replied, "I accept your resignation." If you reach the ultimatum stage, there are other, better ways to handle the situation.

Finally, in discussions with your supervisor, don't compare yourself with a specific person in your work group, for example, "Mary gets the good jobs." This is no way to get a chance to do the work that Mary does. On the other hand, to say "After the monthly payoffs, I would like to work on the correspondence desk for a couple of days" might get you the opportunity to learn the work that Mary does. With a good supervisor, you can gain nothing discussing the work or performance of another specific person. Stick to your own performance and pay, past and future.

THE DOs

How about the DOs? To start with, do assure yourself that you and your supervisor view and evaluate your work similarly. Take the initiative to verify this. Most people don't, but it's an essential basis for work and personal growth. Regardless of your company's review system, do a little preparation, make a few notes, and discuss your performance with your supervisor. Do a neat summary of the recent past and the present, but put your emphasis on the near future, the next six months. Ask for one or several work assignments that represent growth. Specifically mention that you want to learn and perform more valuable work.

How do you talk about your pay goals? Again, this is very much a matter of personal styles—yours and your supervisor's. At a minimum, make statements that relate your job level and pay goals for the next two or three years. You are not asking for a commitment or even an answer. You are expressing your expectations regarding both work opportunity and pay. In the conversation, you are committing for your present and future work contribution. This includes your personal effort for learning—school, training classes, reading, and learning on the job.

THE RIGHT SONG

The right words and tactics in conversations of this type can be keys to major opportunities. If you can provide your supervisor with your plan in the words and style commonly used by managers with whom he or she works, you improve your chances, and your supervisor's, immeasurably. The right words and tactics in such conversations have a powerful effect.

You can learn and play that game; you can learn and use those words and that style. Some you can learn directly from your supervisor. Listen to the words and phrases that he or she uses, including those which he or she brings back from meetings. Understand their structure as your company uses them. If there are written procedures available to you, read them. Carefully—not too obviously—use them in conversations with your peers, with your spouse, or with friends; Get comfortable with the language used by those who are several layers above you. Don't load your conversation with jargon; do become familiar with the words and usages that your superiors use to express their thinking.

A word of caution: Be your own thinker. Have your own opinions. Don't give up your independence and freedom. Expressing your goals and plans in your company's language will give them substantial added value.

When you're discussing your career game with your boss, or with anyone, keep the focus of your conversation on your *work*. With your supervisor, don't hesitate to make an occasional reference to your pay expectations, but attach them to your work expectations. Be careful in talking pay; you may scare your supervisor. He or she may know only a little more than you about the pay game in your company.

CAREER PERSPECTIVE

Visualizing your whole career is like preparing for a long road trip. Visualizing the immediate future is just as easy as planning the routes to nearby cities. Even if you haven't traveled there, you have familiarity and assurance from your contacts with others who have.

In the early years, just knowing that the career roads are open to various directions and higher levels is enough. For the distant years, you rely on your good company, just as you would rely on the routing of a good automobile club for a distant motor trip.

Once you have this perspective, concentrate on planning the present career that your actions are already shaping. When you have worked for a few years, your present career is your work of the next three to eight years.

How can you measure the job growth that you plan in that period? Your measurements will be rough at best, but it's worthwhile to formulate a few.

Look at the jobs beside you and above you. Choose two of these, at least one of them at a higher level, whose work you would want to experience. Don't worry that you might want to change later; for now, consider these jobs a good direction and level for you to be heading toward.

Next, check the pay associated with the jobs that you have picked. Again, this may require discretion and caution. Consider whether these jobs allow enough pay growth in the period you're planning. Conversely, if you think there is too big a gap between your present pay and the pay of the job that you want, you're probably wrong. Go for it!

Regardless of your situation, pin down the work and pay that you want in the next three to eight years. No matter that you may change later; for now, it's clear to you what game you're playing.

8

Learning – The Triple Payoff

You have no choice but to sustain your learning. It's an essential, primary resource of career growth. Learning is unique in producing satisfaction in itself, as well as directly feeding career success. Learning can be a partial substitute for experience. Exploiting your learning is a key to at least three payoffs:

Achieving the two primary career goals – personal fulfillment from more valuable work, confirmed by increasing paychecks.

The innate, mysterious satisfaction of new knowledge itself.

Confirming that you can successfully operate a goal-seeking system by designing and achieving goals of learning.

But misunderstanding how learning operates in contributing to career success can lead to disappointment. There are several fallacies that create troubles:

· Failure to understand the opportunities for learning on the job.

The blind, go-back-to-school impulse.

I've increased my education; now promote me and raise my pay.

LEARNING ON THE JOB

Your work is the greatest learning opportunity of your whole life. Not just because you spend 2000 hours each year at work (far more than you spent at school), but because you've got it all together at work—resources, personal motivation, expectation (your own and your company's), continual opportunity for interaction and application of all you learn, and direct reward.

I speak here not only of the passive sense of learning—receiving knowledge that others have. You must also seek knowledge in its active sense. You must use your work to create new knowledge for yourself and your company. You must look for new ways to apply old knowledge. You must do your share of teaching in your company.

Just understanding this is not sufficient. Do something! You must make a personal plan for learning on the job. It can be a part of a larger plan for personal education. You can't afford to waste this opportunity.

When I discuss this subject, a frequent response is that old, trite saying, "I still learn something new every day." When I hear it, I look at the speaker and think of the old German proverb, "Born dumb, learned nothing, forgot everything." This person does not understand. My on-the-job learning plan for you is no freebie handed to you on a platter, graciously and willingly accepted by you. You have to identify your needs, find resources, set a schedule. In other words, you must plan, and you must take action. It is an essential part of your career plan.

FRUSTRATED BY YOUR CAREER? THEN GO BACK TO SCHOOL

Returning to school will not solve career problems. If you've set a goal and need additional schooling as part of that goal, then returning to school is a good plan.

But it's wrong to return to school in frustration. Yet thousands of people do it, simply because they can't get their careers going. Counselors never say you're not ready for more school; they need you in school; they direct you to what they think is your best-fit course. They may have had the same problem that you have and solved it by giving up on a stalled career. But returning to school is not a blanket solution to a stalled career.

Additional schooling can increase and redirect your resource value. It can give you the benefit of other people's knowledge and experience. Personal contacts made in school can make major contributions to solving your career problems. And in the school environment you may be able to stand back and survey yourself and your company in a way not otherwise possible. Your viewpoint is more distant and your perspective is different. It could be just what you need.

Test and assure yourself before you invest in major additional education. Consider your recent assignments. Are you getting your share of the good ones? If you're being assigned a series of continuing growth challenges, and handling them capably, you may be doing well with the greatest learning resource – on-the-job training.

EDUCATIONAL OBSOLESCENCE

I said earlier that you have no choice but to continue learning in support of your career. Can we measure the truth of that statement? Partially.

Estimates are that the halflife of your present education is anywhere from five to ten years. In that time, half of your present knowledge will have lost its value. Roughly, this means that 5 to 15 percent of your present knowledge loses its value each year. The engineer who was an ace sliderule pusher twenty years ago doesn't take it out of the desk today.

You can't just replace this lost knowledge. You must more than replace it: You must replace it and add enough more to support the real growth of your career. You must even acquire some understanding of the nature of knowledge itself. A part of your learning must be about the basics of new ways to store and process information.

You must sustain your expectation of continuing to learn. Many people are thrilled to realize that learning their work is a more satisfying experience than learning in school.

THE LEARNING PROCESS

I can't give you a guaranteed formula for learning in the career path that you choose, nor can anyone else. But I can offer you understanding of two major processes of learning that will help in your planning. They are not original. The first, "Personal Learning Curves," was explained to me by a bright young contemporary in my first career job. The second, "The Spiral of Learning," was explained in an exciting IBM training course when computers were young.

Personal Learning Curves

When you get a new work assignment, your pace of learning has a definite pattern. Everyone senses the patterns but the patterns are often confused by emotions associated with the new work. When you're bound up in the work, you have a mixture of excitement related to the new prize and a little panic caused by your unfamiliarity with the work.

Your burst of initial, rapid learning is extremely valuable. During this period, both your knowledge and your value as an employee increase rapidly. Your work efficiency may be fairly low, but your investment in learning is high.

In the 1940s, the rhythms of these pulses and waves of learning were expressed in some remarkably simple arithmetic which was first used to manage production of military material. Some minor miracles of performance resulted. More recently, applications of these concepts have produced similar miracles in designing and producing electronic products.

You can use the same concepts to produce some minor miracles of your own career learning.

Figure 8.1 is a graph of the Personal Learning Curve. It illustrates the cumulative learning of a person exposed to a new learning opportunity.

The horizontal axis represents the months of participation. The vertical axis expresses the cumulative amount of learning for that time. The rate of learning corresponds to the slope of the line at that point. In the early months, learning is quite rapid. In the later months, the curve is flatter, indicating slower learning after long exposure. The strong early-learning rate and the associated early accumulation of new knowledge are two points of personal opportunity.

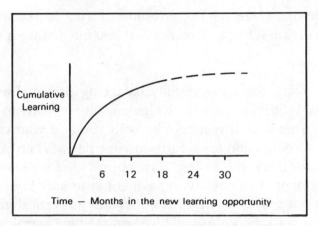

FIGURE 8.1. The personal learning curve.

The time scales for jobs and people are variable—people learn differently; different situations affect the schedule of learning. But all situations and all people are remarkably similar in that people who are qualified for the assignment they're given will consume most of the opportunity to learn how it is done, and its background, in twelve to eighteen months. (This does not include the fact that they may have used the opportunity to create new knowledge or new ways of operating in the job.)

Understanding this concept of learning suggests an obvious personal strategy for learning on the job: Stacked Learning.

Stacked Learning

If you can manage your schedule of job assignments properly, you can double or triple your career learning. Figure 8.2 illustrates this concept of stacked learning. The lowest curve expresses the learning of someone occupying the same assignment for five years. The highest curve expresses the cumulative learning of someone exposed to three learning opportunities during the same period. This is no dream scheme; it works. But you must make it work for you.

Making it work requires carefully balancing personal and company goals. I said that your work efficiency is low early in your assignment. This is an investment by both you and your company. It creates an obligation for return on your part. When you make your plan for stacked learning, it must provide for repayment of this investment. The obvious repayment is to stay longer in the job; that's not what you want. A better way is vertical growth in the same organization; this will give you the next learning opportunity without taking your experience from the organization. Another way is to double up in your work group: Learn the assignment of another person in the same or an associated work group. Then your return of investment can work in parallel to your next learning assignment.

The best way to return the investment is to stay in the work long enough to use your knowledge to rework and improve the way the work is performed. Improve productivity, change the work,

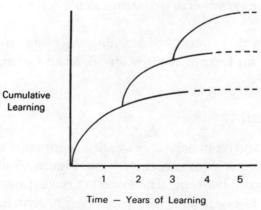

FIGURE 8.2. Stacked learning.

enlarge it, cut its cost, provide more service for the same cost. Leave your mark by devising a better way of doing that job.

Your opportunity to use the concept of stacked learning will depend on your return to the work group that provides the opportunity. It's more a personal than a company problem. It's a specific problem between you and your supervisor. Done right, you will either rise under your supervisor or your supervisor will request that you return when he or she has more challenging assignments.

THE SPIRAL OF LEARNING

The Spiral of Learning is more indirect than Stacked Learning. Using its principles assures the strength of a solid, integrated knowledge base. When The Spiral of Learning was explained to me, it solved some puzzles that recurred throughout my education. For example, I was taught logarithms in the sixth grade, the eighth grade, and again later in high school. I recognized the necessity of repetition, but thought it was overdone.

The Spiral, illustrated conceptually in Figure 8.3, shows a learning path for a manufacturing business. The four broad functional areas are shown as quadrant subjects—create, make, market, and support functions. Keep in mind that these are knowledge groups; they do not portray operations. The quadrant representing knowledge about "make" has been exploded into a typical subject array. Depending on your assignment, you need various amounts of knowledge of these subjects.

The spiral path starting in the center is a rough view of someone beginning to learn the business. The inner loop is initial learning. First exposure to the component subjects is very shallow. But successive loops return to that subject. This is more than just repetition.

In the repeat loops you return with new knowledge of the companion subjects from all quadrants. The reinforcement of related subject knowledge takes hold. You begin to realize that there are gaps in knowledge–both yours and others'. Conflicts become apparent. You are able to argue, to reason, to think, to experiment, not just to receive and to store knowledge.

Having new career goals makes you see gaps and deficiencies in your knowledge. As an engineering student I managed to avoid accounting completely. Later, in a seminar on finance and accounting, I was struck by the similarity of the accounting system to the input-output concepts of engineering. My goal to be a controller was born. But I was lucky. By thinking in input-output concepts, accounting became both attractive and easy to learn. I found that you can learn concepts of accounting with only a minimal knowledge of bookkeeping.

As you develop goals and plans, you need a realistic appraisal of your present knowledge and needs for learning. I don't propose that you make a layout in the spiral format. But you do need a few notes of your specific subject needs.

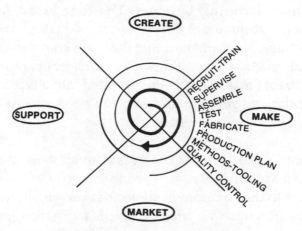

FIGURE 8.3. The spiral of learning.

Watch out for subject "spokes" that are completely missing. Plan how and when you will fill your needs. Keep The Spiral in mind as you plan.

SOURCES

Presently, when you think of learning you think of school. You need to modify that: When you think of learning, think of work and school, in that order.

My first reason is recognition that work and experience are the richest sources of all knowledge. My second reason relates to the different kinds of knowledge. For most of us "school" knowledge is passive knowledge; at best, we confirm it in the laboratory or by exercise. "Work" knowledge is active knowledge; sure, much of it is passive, but even the humblest worker lives with the opportunity to create new knowledge in his or her work. Since we are already oriented to school learning, I'll assign it the second priority. It is the second great source of learning.

On-the-job learning first requires personal observation, reasoning, experimentation, confirmation, and dissemination. But these may follow your efforts to acquire what other people will give you so willingly. Once again, I suggest an active effort.

Identify who has the knowledge you need. Don't seek experts at first. Rather, find someone with whom you communicate well, someone who needs to gain as much as you in an exchange of knowledge. One person is enough, two at most. As you both learn, you can enlarge your contacts, with your associate or alone. Work up to communicating with the experts. Careful! For the exchange to be worthwhile to them, you have to contribute something that they need. You don't have to become an expert in their field, but you should have valuable knowledge in peripheral fields that they need.

Reading is the most essential and easiest source of continuing learning. The lively style of some magazines and trade newspapers are my favorites. Sometimes you must wade into a book or published paper for a long-term look at the future of your work. Don't think that you have to understand all or most of what you read. In many cases, 20 percent comprehension will introduce an idea that you would otherwise never encounter. Stay over your head in your reading. Discuss what puzzles you with your peers and with experts you know. Keep up with at least one weekly news or business magazine; you need its wider viewpoint.

VIEWPOINT

Your viewpoint has a significant effect on learning and growth. Many people view their work with head bent down. By this I mean that they see their own work plus only a limited amount of what's going on in the rest of the company. If you intend to grow and rise at all, you have to develop a broader viewpoint that includes your new position.

Many people who limit their viewpoint become expert in their work, but only in the narrowest sense. Often they are frustrated because they know they are experts and wonder why they aren't selected for promotion. Their personal feeling is usually reinforced by comments like, "Harry, we don't know what we'd do without you in this job." Don't worry about it; Harry will be there forever.

View the organization of your company as a pyramid. Make the effort to understand its products, its operations, and its organization from a viewpoint several levels above your job. You must display this kind of understanding and concern to be a candidate for growth.

Don't stop there. You need contact with the outside world to see where your career fits into the world.

HOW MUCH TIME?

Learning is my second and last 2 percent program for you. You must dedicate at least 2 percent of your work time to a deliberate personal plan for learning, for renewing and increasing your present knowledge.

I usually get two strong, opposite reactions to this proposal. To those who say, "I can't make that much time available," I reply, "I don't believe you." The other common reaction is, "2 percent just isn't enough; it should be at least 5 percent." I reply, "Just give me the 2 percent on a deliberate, sustained basis. Then we will discuss increasing it to 3 percent or 5 percent."

My program means that you define the subjects that you need, to update your existing knowledge or to enter a new field. It means setting a time for exploring these subjects by reading, personal contacts, or formal instruction. It means asking yourself annually whether you are dedicating 40 hours each year to learning specifically identified subjects on a scheduled basis.

PRIORITIES VERSUS ALLOCATIONS

Don't confuse priorities and allocation of time. Give learning an urgent priority but allocate a small amount of your time to it. Whatever percentage you allocate for learning, you must use it on a continuing basis. You can wait until the end of the day or the end of the week, but you can't wait until the end of the month or when your current project is complete.

Since your managed learning will involve different resources, those resources will have to be used on different schedules. Learning from contacts at work has to be scheduled when you and your contacts have time. Learning from reading provides the most flexible schedule—but is the one most subject to procrastination. Formal schooling is the most postponable.

BREAKOUT—FOURTH-LEVEL LEARNING

How do you handle an urgent need for learning, one directly coupled to being successful in a new assignment? To describe this situation, I use the term "fourth level," not as a buzzword but to emphasize a major new phase of career learning.

You can loosely regard high school as level one. College or extensive, basic work orientation is level two. Level three is when you advance to specific application and confirmation of advanced work skills; degree or not, this is the equivalent of a master's degree.

After that you break out; you move beyond basic texts to apply advanced skills, sensitive to particular needs in your own company environment. You are at the point of personal need to influence your company's work and systems of work.

Let me illustrate this with an example of a young man who has just received a promotion. Knowledge is a minor but important part of his problem. He knows it. He has had a vertical promotion, has kept his old responsibility, and has risen to major responsibilities that are new and unfamiliar to him. It was an unexpected promotion, so he's standing with a surprise package in his hands. He knows this promotion is different from his previous ones. It is a breakout for him. He has a massive need for new knowledge, but a lot of his previous experience still applies.

This promotion moved him past the point where he shared much of the operating work. Now his work is dominated by management tasks. He is occupied with new, unfamiliar requirements. He attends regular management meetings. He is expected to understand the operating reports from many areas that are used at high levels to assess company performance. He interacts with managers who have long familiarity with the operating reports that are new to him, whereas he has limited understanding of his own reports and no understanding of their related reports.

He's beginning to classify what he must learn. Some things he needs to learn quickly. How? A cooperative, encouraging predecessor. Since that person also has limited time, he must design their contacts to get the maximum transfer of knowledge.

But he also sees and discusses his more remote needs. For instance, business finance has always seemed obtuse and remote to him. He's eager to connect that kind of knowledge to the assets for which he is now responsible. Yesterday that kind of interest was remote.

He knows that these and other elements of management skills have to be identified and priorities set for learning. However, most of these needs are minor priorities. The primary push—the major allocation of his time—has to be devoted to today's work. He has to go out and meet with his new people. He designs these contacts for maximum learning. He tries to learn with discrimination, not just to accept old attitudes and methods. So he tucks information away with questions, to flag it for challenging later. He's tuned to the ideas and questions raised by his new contacts.

EASY, WRONG SOLUTION

Don't mistakenly diagnose your career problem as lack of knowledge or education. Most people know a great deal more than they give themselves credit for. By far, the most common problem is that you don't understand how to use the knowledge that you already have. This comes from not knowing how to use the people in your company for your common good. Misdiagnosis invites the easy, wrong solution: Go back to school. First, get your career basics, your goals, straightened out—*then* go back to school if necessary.

9

Innovation— Great Test of Learning

Whenever you speak, you pour forth a stream of innovation. The sentences and intonations of human speech, the combinations of thoughts and sounds, put together in your brain, and shaped by your speech organs, are so complex that no scientist, no computer, can explain their complexity. You have a need to communicate, and you use a set of mental and physical resources so powerful, so subtle, so sophisticated, that no one yet understands how the process works. But, we all do it. And as those with whom we talk operate similar systems, thoughts and ideas are created with this same incredible complexity.

But you tell me that you can't innovate!

You write a little poetry, an accomplishment even more complex than basic, communicative speech. When you speak, you use metaphors—association of unlike things—a process that some think may be the very essence of thinking and knowledge. This earns you the envy of the computer designer.

You may like making new recipes or changing old ones. You sketch a little. You have created the best-looking yard on the block. And you still say that you can't innovate.

I say that you CAN innovate! I say that you DO innovate, continually.

Innately, we seem to resist the idea that innovation can come from modest sources—you and me. I call this the "Little-Ol'-Me Syndrome." Generally, we refuse to classify our own small creations as innovations. We try to think of innovations as the great thoughts or acts of great persons.

I could illustrate by pointing out that Einstein developed his breakthrough theories while very young, working in a modest job as a postal clerk. The Wright brothers built their aeroplane—engine and all—in their bicycle shop. Henry Ford had similar beginnings.

I prefer a more meaningful illustration. The most prolific stream of innovation I have participated in and read about, pours from our American armed forces in the breadth and depth of its operations:

> Our infantry is stalled, with heavy casualties, by the hedgerows of rural France. A sergeant, with a welder, converts tanks to 'dozers, breaches the obstacles, and our advance resumes.

* * *

> Unexpected bitter winter and late shipments of gloves bring frozen operations and frostbite. A few GIs, with donated

sewing machines and blankets, create warm gloves in quantity, and operations resume.

* * *

A bored military, waiting on a Pacific isle, has no clean laundry. An idea, a few oil drums, and soon makeshift wind-driven washing machines have taken over the washing chore.

All of those things involved hardware. How about the ideas, the different ways of doing things, a way of doing something we couldn't do before—the "software"? Schemes clever beyond belief seemed to burst forth to meet every need. Consider a small area, the kitchen:

Sergeant Kuntz, a mess sergeant so clever that he had an all-volunteer kitchen crew, created bean sandwiches; they filled a need. And he traded coffee grounds to a farmer for fresh eggs; the farmer hadn't tasted real coffee for five years.

Innovations come from everywhere and everyone. They seem to be contagious. They involve basic things like cooking, subtle changes to complex equipment by unsubtle people, make-dos when the regular channels of supply fail. Many enable mission performance when failure would be completely justified. Some are for personal comfort. And most of these things happen in the most rigid, structured, disciplined, organizational environment, at all levels.

THE MOTIVATORS

Innovation *happens* when people drive themselves to achieve goals which they accept. Their goals may be self-set or assigned. They may share them with a group, or work solo. This is the case of the tankdozers and the gloves.

Innovation *happens* when people are *bored*. When they are either energetic, or intelligent and have nothing to drive for, they invent something to do. It may be the idle brain and the devil's workshop, but they do something. This is the case of the windmill washing machine.

THE KILLER

Innovation *doesn't happen* when people let themselves be consumed by administration tasks. Administrative work is effective and the goal is justified—"Keep on crankin', bunkie." Perhaps they are even exploiting a previous innovation. This is a false sense of security. It is the great usurper of the opportunity for innovation. Excessive administration is like being possessed by a silent, consuming demon. There is no better analysis of it than C. Northcote Parkinson's book, *Parkinson's Law*. If you are consumed by endless administrative duties, take time to read it; use it as a mirror. If you can't make some time available for personal innovation, you have surrendered your freedom.

Bored or busy, you must make time for innovation. It's a part of the process. You have no choice. But when you're consumed by the administrative rat race, finding time for innovation is tough. Only when you stop long enough to recognize your situation will you commit to do what is necessary.

I worked with a cost accountant who could never catch up—he was a hard worker, but he was always three months behind. I had to force him to abandon three months of backlog and work on current information; I locked the file and took the keys. It was like shattering an idol. He couldn't believe that no one missed the information for the lost period; all he heard were compliments for current data.

FORCED INNOVATION

Only a few innovations are simple discoveries. We stumble across new knowledge, or someone offers us the solution to a persistent problem. Those cases are rare, and they're a joy.

Nearly all innovation results from deliberate assault on a problem. That sounds formidable, but it's only a little different from the way you attack a crossword puzzle. The trigger is simply recognition of the problem and the decision to solve it. The responsive innovation—the solution—often starts with your attempts to define just what the problem is.

Innovation is a combination of problems, opportunities, problem solving, and productivity improvements. It also includes the uncounted small improvements that you add to your daily work habits.

WHAT KIND OF INNOVATIONS?

The kinds of innovation I want you to apply in your work are low-keyed, personal, pervasive, persistent, and captivating ones that you incorporate in the flow of your daily activities. "Low-keyed" because you may never conceive the blockbuster, the big one. Don't wait for it. Go for the dozens, the hundreds, of small things that you can quietly change. "Personal" because you must at least start by doing it yourself. "Persistent" to keep up the unrelenting, low-keyed search for better ways and more satisfaction. "Captivating," because you should acquire and adopt the innovations of others. You thus support and reinforce them through your applications. "Pervasive" ones are the application of many small changes into operations, or even products, where you have the opportunity.

LEARNING AND INNOVATION

Used well, learning and innovation are inseparable. Passive learning stands apart from innovation; it enables you to perform and understand things established by others.

But active learning is the companion and motivation of innovation. As you move in your Spiral of Learning with active learning, you carry this companion spiral of innovation, the association of that new knowledge with its generated innovation. Working like this, living like this, becomes a change in your personal habit, a new part of your personal style.

At first, if you have an impulse to start a program of innovation by joining with someone, don't. This is another thing you have to at least start by yourself. Tie it to your plan for learning. Provide some checks to make yourself recognize that you are, or are not, using and improving your ability to innovate. Your improvement will create ties between your knowledge and its application in innovation. Again, you don't have to reach for the blockbusters. Go after the large number of small changes that represent minor improvements. If later you confirm your ability to implement your own plan for innovation, then join with others.

FEAR OF FAILURE

Fear of failing has to be one of the greatest obstacles to innovation. No one wants to be laughed at, chided, or even punished for an idea that doesn't work.

But you have innumerable opportunities to try for improvements that don't even have to be visible until they do work. For example, I work with many people who use both calculators and computers. When I introduced some workers to programmable calculators, they began asking questions about their present calculators. Later they asked about some of the more specialized functions that they had never used. They were surprised at how helpful these functions could be in their work. More important, I think, they were surprised at how easily they learned them. Nearly all had mind-sets turning off their abilities to learn. Two different factors were working together here. Both were obstacles to learning and innovation. Ignorance denied the use of an excellent tool. And fear that they couldn't learn perpetuated the ignorance.

We often mistake our ignorance—a simple lack of knowledge—for stupidity, the inability to learn. This tendency is more prevalent among people in lower-level jobs; it's a real deterrent to reaching the higher levels.

Most of us have ideas for solving our work problems but we are reluctant to attempt the solution ourselves. In the case of the programmable calculators, the people could not conceive of asking for a new, $300 machine. I think they were afraid that they couldn't learn how to use it. Their work involved constant calculation that could be performed faster and better with more advanced equipment. The payoff for the small investment would be very fast. What was more important was that they could make their work more satisfying and valuable. My concern in such cases is that so few people realize that today's method will actually decrease in value tomorrow.

What's your choice? It is whether to use your ability to innovate and grow, or to be dragged, kicking and screaming, into tomorrow's world.

THE MOOD OF CHANGE

It is satisfying to work in a group or company which encourages change. I have enjoyed this privilege for a whole career, with minor exceptions. But even in the best situations there are enclaves where the opposite is true. I'm not sure how these islands can exist, but they do. Encouraging people in these areas to show initiative is much like fomenting rebellion. Inevitably, there are wails and weeping and cries of woe. They are best summarized by, '"They' won't let us do it," or "We don't get the *management support* we must have." Hogwash! With a little anxiety, I always throw this right back.

There is no "they." *You* have to find ways. You have to scheme, if necessary, to get it done. You have to define the problem. You have to create the solution. Most important, you have to implement it and keep it working. Management doesn't support you; you support management. Management has its hands full getting the resources you need, watching the competition, allocating the resources, identifying where the train is about to jump the track, and so forth. Management wants you to take initiative in your job and innovate where it is essential to staying competitive. You are capable of doing this, and your personal success depends on your doing it. Further, if you don't do it now you will probably never do it, at any other time, in any other place.

Innovation is literally *contagious*. If you don't attempt your own innovations, you tend to resist those of other people. It becomes difficult not to regard them as threats to your own work. When you switch over, you not only add one innovator, you also eliminate one foot-dragger. This is the contagion—the double lever—and personal satisfaction and pay always come with it.

THE SPIRAL OF LEARNING

Tying innovation to the spiral of learning is a reminder that everything can be improved over and over again. In each successive loop, you add new knowledge and new perspectives. Innovations appear to be reversals of previous improvements. Many examples exist in manufacturing. For instance, a machine designer invents a large, versatile machine that allows tasks that were previously dispersed in several work centers to be combined effectively. A few years later a new machine—smaller, more specialized, but lower in cost—comes along. Using it permits the work to be dispersed again, returned to the people who are closer to the product.

These repeated cycles of improvement are related to the personal learning curves already discussed. The improvements tend to get smaller as the more obvious opportunities are used. However, it's not unusual in the process to have major changes erupt and initiate another rapid cycle of change. All too often these eruptions come from a new participant or from a competitor.

MANAGEMENT QUALITY AND OPPORTUNITY

There are two managements receptive to your personal innovation—good management and bad management. Good management pushes you to innovate—expects you to innovate—both for the company's needs and for your need for personal growth. Bad management generally does not expect you to innovate. Oddly enough, you may have a better opportunity for personal innovation in a bad management situation.

For instance, assume there are obvious problems in your work and you need a different approach. In this situation, your obstacles are lack of time and diversion of attention: You're so busy putting out fires that you can't develop and implement solutions to the problems. Sometimes there's another obstacle, suppression of innovation: Your innovation can be a threat to an incompetent supervisor.

You can overcome the obstacles to innovation under bad management. (Don't take this as saying that you can correct the bad management situation.) Be careful, but get going on the program. Define the opportunities that you want to improve. At the same time, appraise the political situation and the reception that you will get for your innovations. Don't try to correct the problems of the world; just focus on the things in your work that you can change as you learn the game. This is your program to improve your work.

You will do this only if you commit to a date by which you will identify problems that you can solve in your work. You must take some time to play this as a personal game. You must stand back and decide what problems you want to solve.

COMING OUT OF THE CLOSET

I have pushed you to recognize that you do innovate. I have urged you to free yourself from the drug of administrative burden and create a personal, undercover program for innovation within your own job. This concealment, or limited visibility, practically guarantees that you will win without risk.

I know that you will succeed with this approach. When you achieve that success, I urge that you consider expanding your innovation beyond your own job. Open up to join with others. These extensions can be both solo and with groups. By solo I don't mean that you do it all by yourself, but that you should champion innovation—propose and help implement changes that reach beyond your job. Being a champion means that you accept risk and share responsibility for change and effective growth in your company. This is the real game, the real satisfaction, the real reward.

BIG CHANGES

I push you to develop the habit of innovation. This keeps you in the mood, makes innovation a part of your daily work. You start the change when you stop thinking of innovation as being associated primarily with new product concepts. You begin to see improvement opportunities in methods, organization, boredom, routine, waste, useless duplication, bad working conditions, underutilized people, underutilized machines, and so forth.

Regardless of whether your innovations bring big change, your attitude for change becomes a foundation for your career growth. However, I do see people who grow from the small-change habit to influencing systems larger than they ever imagined. Each of the cases I will describe could be one of these types.

The first case concerns a man who was invited to join an improvement team. He may have suggested the formation of the team or he may have asked to join. The teams were free to select their projects for improvement. Their dual purpose was to learn the improvement system and to create improvements as they learned. I don't know how much of the man's project was conceived before he joined the team, but he convinced the team to adopt his project. Some were familiar with the organizations and work affected; some were not.

I think the magnitude of his proposal shocked his team members: He proposed changes in organization and work that promised to save nearly a quarter million dollars annually. (Generally, teams of this type concentrate on the learning experience; they view with pride projects that save a few thousand dollars.)

His suggestion was an extension of work that was already started. Several years previously an assembly supervisor had centralized all part preparation in his department. By concentrating all of this type of work for all departments, he achieved major economies of scale. Methods and skill improved. He was able to use better equipment. Engineers were encouraged to use standard designs and increase the volume scale of fewer types. Other departments observed these improvements and followed suit.

The innovator proposed the next step: combination of the sections into a service department. He steered his team into detailed methods study, equipment selection, and layout design. Together they recognized the disadvantages of moving the operations farther from the primary assembly. They concluded that it was justified by the savings. Over several months, they designed new methods and layouts. They made estimates of times and costs. They made organization tables, before and after, including names of all the people affected. They confirmed that new jobs were available for each of the more than twenty people who were affected by the change. Throughout the design of the changes and the calculation of their savings, all of the people were kept aware that their innovation was an essential element of the continuing competition in their markets.

Along with other teams, they presented their proposal for upper-management review. They were challenged, and they answered questions. They were privileged to hear the management discussion and decision on the spot. This is unusual and a real compliment to the work of the proposer and the team.

Few innovations are so clean-cut. It is unusual to have both prompt decisions and execution. The interplay between the originator and the team was similarly clean. For the originator, this was a significant career step. It was an opportunity for him to exercise himself in a department-level challenge. For the others, it was a dramatic introduction to the kind of innovations that all companies need.

BOTH SIDES OF INNOVATION

The principal player in the next case primarily played a lone game. As he developed an administrative management system, he was aware that it filled a primary, new need but also infringed on an existing system. I use the term "system" to mean the work of a group of people, not machines or computers.

My opening reference to "both sides of innovation" is meant to emphasize that many innovations have opponents as well as proponents. In retrospect, successful changes tend to look clear-cut and simple; but prior to implementation there are usually major opposition and objections. Consider the roles of actors in this play, as viewed by the principal:

Principal. The system designer, who conceived the system as an "Underground Project." Now he's out in the open, selling, dedicated to what he sees as a major improvement.

Embedded Functional Group. Largely professionals, operating a doctrinaire system costing well over $100,000 per month. It's the only show in town offering the service.

Decentralized Users. The people to whom the system furnishes services. They are skeptical of any centrally furnished system; so each area operates a bootleg, under-the-table system for its real management control.

Ancillary Users. Every system has them. They use the system when they want to but can do without, but feel that anything would be better than the existing anarchy.

Managers. The new central services manager came from operations; most managers trust him, in spite of their people's skepticism.

How does the action go in this shootout? The EFG (Embedded Functional Group) is tall in the saddle, super-confident like all EFGs. After all, they were created from on high five years ago. The idea of being replaced by innovation is inconceivable to them. "Certainly, Principal, you may observe our whole operation. We have nothing to hide." (A little whistling as they walk past the graveyard.) "There is no way you can furnish the service we furnish, or perhaps better service, for only 10 percent of our costs."

But Principal disagrees. He's an innovator; he has ideas. He assumes responsibility for designing a strong, simple, compact, inflexible, low-cost system. He simulates the system, mocks up his reports exactly like the real thing, with live data. He prods Users to comment, criticize, and suggest changes. Some are reluctant, some are enthusiastic, but they're hooked. The reports are so realistic that some managers think the system is already operating: "And you can do all this for us and save a quarter million dollars a year?"

Earlier I said that this is a success book, not a win book. This is the exception. EFG lost! They gave up their opportunity for innovation. They closed their eyes and dug in. They could just as easily have seized the initiative for self-renewal, innovation, and growth of their whole system. They could have invited Principal to join them, or even captured him. Think of all the careers displaced because they didn't.

Their group was drawn into the new group, the new system. Eventually, most of them passed on to new associations. They could just as well have gone on to significant new strength and vitality.

SECTION 2

The Money Game

HAP'S LAWS OF PAY

1. The top 1000 workers in the United States earn 100 times minimum pay.

The big wheels earn $800,000 per year. Nominal minimum pay, about $4.00 an hour, is about $8000 per year. That's 100 to 1. About 50 percent of Mr. Big's pay comes from bonuses and other add-ons, which he doesn't get if his company doesn't earn a profit.

2. Average qualified college graduates start their careers earning twice minimum pay.

Seems low, doesn't it? But, put them all together—engineers, teachers, and accountants—and their starting pay averages about $16,000. The currently favored fields—engineering, science, and math—are paid more, generally $20,000 to $30,000. Pay also varies by locations.

3. Ambitious workers earn 15 percent average raises for their first 15 years of work.

About 9 percent of the 15 percent raises is real. It buys food, clothes, cars, and houses. The other 6 percent is inflation and doesn't buy anything. After 15 years, ambitious people earn about four times the pay that new hires starting in the same field are being paid.

4. There are 40 levels of pay or job grades; each ranges 10 percent higher than the preceding level.

Each job grade has a range of pay above and below the mid-level pay assigned to good work in the associated jobs. Thus a salaried job may have full qualification pay of $2000 a month, and range down to $1600 and up to $2400—highest pay for outstanding work.

5. Average worker's real-pay peaks after 20 years, at 80 percent more than the pay of the first year of work.

If you're starting at $20,000 today—and choose to be average—your dollar-pay will be $112,000 in about year 2005 or 2010. It will be okay but new people will be starting at $64,000 in your job by then.

6. Lifetime earnings of average workers equal 75 years of the pay of their first year of career work.

Put inflation aside. Adjust your thinking to realpay, money that buys both necessities and luxuries. Then it's not hard to build a lifetime budget. Try squeezing cars, houses, and college tuition into a lifetime of average pay.

7. Manage your career—work smarter, not longer or harder—and you will earn 25 years of extra pay in your lifetime.

As a minimum, take this easy path—and earn a 30 percent bonus. There's one big danger. When you see how easily success comes, you'll be tempted to go for the whole bit—longer, harder, and smarter.

10

The Pay Opportunity Model

In the United States, we pay our most valued workers about 100 time what we pay our lowest-paid workers. That means that the minimum pay is $8000 per year (about $4.00 per hour), the top tycoons make about $800,000 per year.

But there's a catch!

In one way or another we guarantee the minimum pay. In contrast, we usually fix the big wheel's pay so that only 40 to 50 percent of his or her nearly $1 million is salary. The big wheel only gets the rest if we produce big, sell big, and have big profits. Well, $400,000 isn't bad. But if he or she is used to nearly $1 million, there must be some suffering in the bad years.

Why do you and I care? We're well above the minimum pay and we're not reaching for the big top pay—at least not yet. Does it affect us? It sure does. We care because we all hang together.

I said at first that the high is 100 times the low pay. That's a pretty rough figure, but it's also a fairly accurate one. It was about the same ten years ago and it probably will be the same ten years from now.

Your pay and mine hangs between these two extremes, but we don't want to keep hanging there. We want to *move*—up from the low, closer to the high.

You need to understand that your opportunity for rapid growth in pay exceeds anything that you have yet imagined. Just as I said that you can increase your work contribution big and fast, so can you increase your pay big and fast. Don't misunderstand. This is no rainbow-and-pot-of-goal fantasy; it will take work and a little time. For now, we will evaluate the pay opportunity. In Chapter 12 we will nail down just what this will mean to your total pay for your whole career.

The model of pay opportunity (discussed later, Figure 10.1) is a model of surprises for everyone who works with it. Even executives are surprised. (In audiences, it is apparent from both the facial expressions and the questions; it's interesting to watch people's eyes go to the ceiling as they mentally calculate their own situation, and then, to see their eyes roam the audience, speculating on who's getting what.) There are three surprises:

1. Raises paid to people sustaining good personal growth are much larger and steadier than generally thought.

2. The simplicity of understanding the situation—the information in actual dollars and rates of growth—is readily available and easy to organize.

3. This is the most important: your company has to be giving raises of 10 to 15 percent or more to numbers of your good people. Companies achieving real growth, rather than just renewing themselves, must have many people growing at these rates.

SO WHAT?

When you know the career game early, when you know what par is, you can set your goals accordingly. Regardless of which track you choose, you'll know better the game you're playing. You will understand your team better. You'll understand the language and the problems. You will know what others are achieving.

GO/NO-GO SITUATION

Many actions and decisions of life and work are so-called go/no-go decisions—there is no half-way: You must go for it all, or not go at all. But in some things you can make partial commitments, and enjoy partial benefits. Pay is one of those things.

You can increase your pay goals—and your work goals—to whatever levels you choose. Your choice is not limited to electing only a very high or a very low goal. All of the steps in between are available to you.

Because of this, you can commit for moderate, long-term improvement. Or you can be skeptical and go for a quick, modest trial to confirm that you can do it. Then you can go on from there. This kind of experimentation helps you build a strong foundation for future career actions. Later, when you've proved you can do it, set goals for whatever challenge pleases you.

WHAT? NO DOLLARS?

Pay growth is a mixture of inflation and real increases. Inflation may be high or low, depending on the current economy. But only your real-pay increases will buy the clothes, houses, biscuits, and cars that you need for your family and yourself.

To understand the concept of inflated money, consider factors that compare pay for various key levels of jobs. You already know that the highest pay in the United States is generally 100 times the pay of the lowest-paid work. Similarly, we could say that you want your pay in five years to be some factor, like two times your present pay. At that time, regardless of inflation, you want to be earning twice the amount that people doing your present kind of work are earning.

Considering pay in light of inflation may give you a little personal deflation at first if you compare your pay four or five years ago this way. You may not be as comfortable with your raises and total increase as you were previously.

PEGPOINTS OF PAY

The extreme ranges of pay that I mentioned at first are real, but their gap is too large to relate to realistic personal goals for most people. You need to understand pay at points closer to the pay you earn now and hope to earn soon. If you understand levels of pay for work between the extreme levels already mentioned, you will understand the rates you will earn in the immediate future years.

Reconsider the two extremes. Our practical lowest common pay is probably a little above the federal minimum pay rate. In the 1970s, this grew from about $2.00 per hour to about $3.00 per hour. This hourly rate can be converted to an annual or monthly rate by multiplying by about 2000 or 170, respectively. Thus $4.00 per hour converts to about $8000 or $9000 per year (depending on overtime and other variables), or about $680 per month.

The pay of top executives grows with inflation, just as low pay does, but their pay is more complicated. In addition to their primary salary, they receive other elements of income, which are usually dependent on performance.

Executive "add-ons" or "perks" are a mixture of short- and long-range goodies. Short-range ones are usually bonuses and outright awards of company stock. The long-range ones, supposedly to strengthen ties with the company, are usually options for stock to be bought at favorable prices and other conditions. These are incentives to improve performance, and get their company's stock prices up.

Now look at pegpoints closer to most of our work and pay—present and future—to build a meaningful model of pay opportunity. Each pegpoint is a general job level associated with a general pay level. First, I want to define pay for two in-between levels of the model to give the model the continuity that it needs.

QUALIFIED COLLEGE GRADUATE

Call the lower in-between level "Qualified College Graduate"(QCG). This general level of work is meaningful because nearly all of you have achieved, or can achieve, the level of work performance that the term expresses, regardless of actual formal education. For many of us, this is our starting level. Since starting college graduates are paid a wide range of salaries, the term defines a general level, an average for more than a half-milion graduates annually.

The composition of pay rates for QCGs varies from year to year as demand for the various educational disciplines varies. In some years accountants and finance majors are in short supply; in others, engineers may be favored with high starting salaries.

Generally, starting salaries for graduates with good qualifications in the most favored fields are about 50 percent higher than the average of all fields. Some skills in short supply may be offered 100 percent more—particularly if the applicant is exceptional, or from a favored college. But what factor can be used on the scale between the high and low?

Qualified College Graduates Are Paid Twice the Minimum Pay Rate, Which Is the Bottom of the Scale

If the going minimum rate is $5.00 per hour, you can expect that the average rate paid all college graduates will be about $20,000 per year. This surprises many people until they remember that most college graduates have chosen fields that pay considerably less than the usually favored fields such as engineering, computer science, and financial control and investment.

Other factors are also acting to determine the rates. Higher degrees of education, such as Masters and PhDs, each bring an additional 10 percent.

LIMIT OF NORMAL AMBITION

The last job level needed to sketch out the pay opportunity model is the toughest to get. The three pay levels already given are well recognized. Their salaries are discussed fairly often in surveys and comments published in newspapers and magazines.

Our in-between but higher-level job is "Limit of Normal Ambition" (LNA). It would be good to have a defined job, or group of jobs such as department manager, superintendent, or director of engineering, but LNA has to represent all of that general level of work. These jobs demand high contribution, balanced among application, knowledge, and responsibility. Those high demands are reflected in the title—these are people just below the executive level. Above this level, the *price you pay* increases severely, enough to limit the attraction for most people.

Developing the pay factor for these near-executives is difficult. Specialized professional magazines give some guidance in their periodic surveys. The best background comes from companies' annual reports that tell the pay of their top executive group: Back out the pay given for the few highest execs, and the average of what's left is a little higher than the Limit of Normal Ambition. Kidding a little, you can classify these people by the size of their briefcases—LNAs usually have briefcases about four inches wide.

Most people guess that LNAs earn about 65 to 75 percent of the pay of the lesser executives. A few calculations of this type indicate that limit-of-normal-ambition jobs earn about 3.5 to 3.7 times the pay of Qualified College Graduates when they are first promoted to their LNA jobs. These factors may seem to be overly precise, but they seem to be both accurate and stable.

Now we have the four primary pay factors that express the range limits of pay, and give good, brief coverage inside the range. Remember that they express the relations between pay for levels of work at any given time.

Now, summarize the relations of these factors:

> Top executives earn about 100 times minimum pay. Of this, about 40 to 50 percent is salary. The balance varies with performance—theirs and their company's.

> Minimum pay is basic, strongly influenced by the federal minimum wage rate.

> Qualified College Graduates are paid about twice minimum pay.

> Pay for limit-of-normal-ambition jobs is 3.6 times the pay of Qualified College Graduates.

These last two points are most important to us because they bracket the pay area in which most of us work.

THE CAREER PAY TRIP

Assume that someone's career path starts as a Qualified College Graduate and grows to the Limit of Normal Ambition. How long does such a trip take?

Some say fifteen years in a good, growing company. Others may say that it's two or three years less than that. Then, if I make this trip and increase my real pay 3.6 times in 15 years, a little calculation indicates that the annual increase of my pay is 9% for those years of growth.

But there's something missing—*inflation*! The whole structure creeps up or leaps up with inflation. When thinking in terms of dollar growth instead of real-pay growth, a factor for annual inflation must be added. How much? In the 1950s inflation was about 2 percent per year. In the 1960s it was 3 percent, but jumping at the end. In the 1970s it was about 7 percent, but it was really jumping at the end of that decade. For the 1980s it has been nearly zero. Again, how much?

In spite of past double-digit inflation, I will use an optimistic 6 percent average inflation for our discussion. Adding this to the real-pay growth, people making this career trip must be earning average pay increases of 15 percent over the period of growth— 9 percent real-pay growth, plus 6 percent inflation.

THE MODEL

Figure 10.1 arranges these factors as a simple model. It uses the job level of QCG as the basis of the factors. The other factors are expressed as ratios to it. Trace the factors in the model and confirm that they express the same relationships that I summarized in the preceding section.

RELATIONSHIPS AMONG JOB GRADES

Pay ranges for each of the next-higher job grades have similar patterns. But each respective point in the next-higher job grade steps up some similar percentage higher than the preceding lower grade. How much should these step up, and how many salaried job levels should there be below executive salary levels?

Try using ten salaried job grade levels, each stepping up 10 percent. Make calculations on this basis and diagram the pay structure that it produces. Figure 11.1 illustrates a typical salary pay scale. Check the upper ranges. The 3.5 pay factor for the top salaried level, S10, is slightly low compared to the 3.6 factor I developed previously for the limit-of-normal-ambition job, but it is good for this illustration.

Note the dollar examples in the figure. If the entry-level pay for a college grad is $1500 per month, the Department Head job would have a top pay of $5250 per month. This confirms that the rough factors are a reasonable base for sample pay structure.

Now extend the factors in the figure to a full pay schedule of the dollar ranges for all ten of the salaried jobs below executive level.

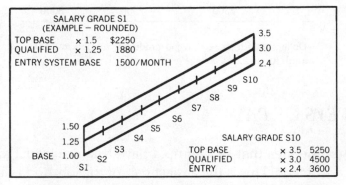

FIGURE 11.1. Salary pay structure—factor basis.

Normally, the midpoints are the basis of the whole pay structure since they represent a fully qualified job occupant. Usually, the midpoints are calculated first, but you can start at any point to build the pay structure. Then set the high and low ranges for each job grade at 20 percent above and 20 percent below the midpoint, respectively.

Table 11.1 illustrates a typical full, salary pay schedule. Its basis is $2000 per month for the low rate of job grade S1, a level that will probably be prevalent in the late 1980s. All calculations were made accurately and then rounded, using a little arbitrary judgment.

TABLE 11.1. Salaried Pay Schedule[a]

Job Grade	Minimum Qualification	Full Qualification Midpoint	Top Premium
S10	4720	5890	7070
S9	4290	5360	6430
S8	3900	4870	5850
S7	3540	4430	5310
S6	3220	4030	4830
S5	2930	3660	4390
S4	2660	3330	3990
S3	2420	3030	3630
S2	2200	2750	3300
S1	2000	2500	3000

[a] Dollars/month, based on job grade S1, minimum $2000/month for qualified college graduate.

SURVEYS OF PAY

Don't get the idea that setting up a pay structure is just an exercise in arithmetic. This is the easiest part of the job, and is actually the last part.

No company can set up its pay schedules simply by a process of arithmetic. What any company can pay its people is determined by its markets; markets for its products determine what it can afford to spend for labor; markets for labor where it recruits its people determine the rates it has to pay for the kind of good people it needs.

A survey of pay requires extensive preparation. Companies participating in the same labor market must be identified and queried. Key jobs that are common among the companies must be identified. There must be a good understanding of employee benefits and their relation to compensation.

As in many things, the rationale of the markets results in patterns which are expressed in the organization of pay rates and jobs in the pay schedules. Some of the patterns are so fundamental that distortions are quickly detected. Several years ago, one of the business magazines described a near-revolt of people in mid-salaried jobs. In prior years, pay rates for low-paying jobs and high-paying jobs had advanced beyond those of the middle ranks. This had distorted the pay curves into a sort of soup bowl—higher on both ends than in the middle. Management had to respond to the complaints of people in those jobs and gradually correct the middle rates.

This essential background for setting up fair and competitive pay scales for a company is laid by conducting surveys and analysis. Using this information, combined with the company's policies for pay, it maintains salaries that attract and motivate good people.

ILLUSTRATIONS

Let's see how these pay concepts apply to two typical job families. Our careful process of job evaluation has determined that pay for an engineering job family can be fairly administered using three job grades, as follows:

	Grade	Low	Mid	High
Senior engineer	S6	$2900	$3620	$4350
Engineer	S4	$2400	$3000	$3600
Junior engineer	S2	$1980	$2480	$2970

Similarly, evaluations for accountants are:

	Grade	Low	Mid	High
Senior accountant	S5	$2640	$3300	$3960
Accountant	S3	$2180	$2730	$3270
Junior accountant	S1	$1800	$2250	$2700

For both of these job families, the highest pay is more than 100 percent above the lowest pay. In the evaluation of the two families, the work of the engineers ranked slightly higher than the work of the accountants. Practically, the opportunities for pay and growth are very similar.

COMPLETING THE PAY STRUCTURE

Using these same concepts, the pay structure for salaried jobs can be extended downward to organize pay for jobs paid on an hourly basis. After that, extending the schedule higher provides the structure for executive jobs.

For each of these two extensions, start by adding the midpoints of pay for ten more jobs above and below the salaried range I selected to start the illustrations in the preceding section. Each steps up or down by the factor I elected to use between jobs in the salaried range. The extended ranges are illustrated in the complete pay structure (see Figures 11.2*a* and 11.2*b*).

Hourly Pay

As illustrated in Figure 11.2*a*, extending the midpoint line downward from the salaried jobs defines the fully qualified pay line for the hourly jobs. Note that the highest-paid hourly job grade, H10, coincides with the lowest-paid salaried job grade, S1. In real systems, there are usually several overlapping job grades.

The pay ranges above and below full qualification are usually smaller than the ranges for salaried jobs. In many companies, the movement of hourly paid workers upward through their pay range is based primarily on time in a particular job. Jobs are often more structured and premium contribution by the workers may result in assignment to the next job level.

The lowest range may be clipped at the bottom, indicating that the lowest entry jobs are for a qualification period from which recruits move quickly to higher job grades.

The pay factors shown agree with the general concepts first discussed in the pay opportunity model. The lowest-range factor is a little higher than the federal minimum pay rate. The lowest pay factor for midpoint is 0.53 for H1. This could be used for an initial raise after a period of a few weeks or months.

Executive Pay

Job grades E1 thru E10, as shown in Figure 11.2*a*, represent pay factors which will cover all executives except the highest-paid officers for the largest companies. For example, the top five or ten executives of half of the Fortune 500 companies are paid more than the factors indicated at the top of Figure 11.2*a*. Note that the upper lines are broken, indicating the possibility for extension to cover these important executive jobs.

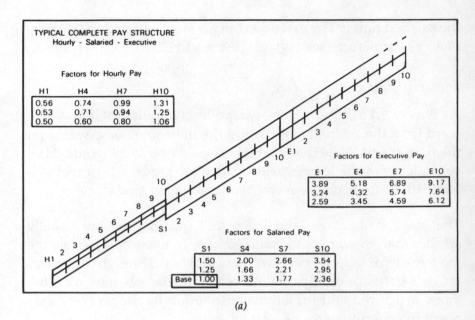

The figure contains the following tables:

TYPICAL COMPLETE PAY STRUCTURE
Hourly - Salaried - Executive

Factors for Hourly Pay

H1	H4	H7	H10
0.56	0.74	0.99	1.31
0.53	0.71	0.94	1.25
0.50	0.60	0.80	1.06

Factors for Executive Pay

E1	E4	E7	E10
3.89	5.18	6.89	9.17
3.24	4.32	5.74	7.64
2.59	3.45	4.59	6.12

Factors for Salaried Pay

	S1	S4	S7	S10
	1.50	2.00	2.66	3.54
	1.25	1.66	2.21	2.95
Base	1.00	1.33	1.77	2.36

(a)

Factor for Qualified College Graduate equals 1.00 (Designated base salary – S1)

Factors for midpoint rates step up 10% per job grade.

Ranges of pay for job grades:

Salaried and executive	up 20% – down 20%
Hourly	up 5% – down 15%

Assume the rate for qualified graduate (base) is \$1800/month:

	Low	Mid	High	
Executive job grade E1	4660	5830	7000	\$/mo.
Hourly job grade H4	1080	1278	1332	\$/mo.
	6.23	7.37	7.68	\$/hr.

(b)

FIGURE 11.2.(a) Typical complete pay structure; (b) basis of pay structure and dollar example.

This extension applies to the same top executives discussed in the Pay Opportunity Model. You will find, with a little arithmetic, that extending this pay structure upward ten more job grades for this group matches the pay factors and dollar salaries discussed in that model. Then the chairperson of the board, the president, executive VPs, and all of the other super-VPs of the largest companies would be covered.

Are such lofty jobs actually covered by the pay structure? Generally, yes—if for no other reason than to provide for conformance to a possible government wage and salary control. In the past, under such conditions, companies which could show that changes in executive salaries conformed with an equitable system were allowed some flexibility in pay administration.

If the pay structure in Figure 11.2a were converted to a total pay schedule, it would be a complete map of basic salaries required to plan a career path for pay. But if your goal is to rise to the higher executive levels, you must extend the upper end of the pay structure.

The highest job illustrated, E10, applies to the president of a moderate size company, or vice-president of a larger company. For example, the pay factors for E10 range from 6.1 to 9.2. In a year when the going rate for Qualified College Graduates is $20,000, you would expect the salary for the president of a small- to moderate-sized company to range from $120,000 to $135,000 per year. Vice-presidents of very large companies would earn the same range of salaries.

BONUSES AND THE OTHER GOODIES

Bonuses are often understood better by those outside of companies than by those inside. Many people inside regard the system for bonus pay as so secret as to be discussed only in low voices with close associates. Some information has always been available in business publications. Recently, more disclosures have resulted from the dictates of securities control agencies.

The most encouraging development currently is the frankness of companies to encourage and broaden extraordinary contributions of employees by the extraordinary pay that bonuses represent. For example, in a turnaround situation in a major company, a new executive was shocked at the narrowness and distortion of bonus performance incentive among key employees. The changes he initiated extended participation from about 100 to more than 1200 people—he may be a person who gets commensurate results.

If your company publishes annual statements and basic data on compensation of officers, you can extend this information into some understanding of your bonus system. In some cases, internal publications and stockholder communications sketch a fairly complete picture. Few people develop this information for understanding the pay opportunity offered by their company's bonus plan. Consider a case.

Your company has 100,000 employees, as noted in its annual report. From its mixture of Create-Make-Market, you can guess that 20 percent of the employees are salaried and are in groups most likely to produce the kind of work that deserves bonus consideration. Further, only about half of those people will produce any innovation or extraordinary performance that makes them candidates for bonuses. Public data state that 2500 people were paid bonuses in the past year.

Do you realize the magnitude of the opportunity for you that is expressed by this information? It implies that one out of four qualified people made the extraordinary contribution that earned a bonus! What marvelous odds to work with!

This is just an illustration. Your own company will be different. Its opportunity may be more or less than the illustration. What's your approach if you want to get in the game? Consider two approaches.

The first is old faithful—simple excellence in your work. This one you must do, but the second is more interesting. Define a triumph in your work that is needed by your company—preferably an innovation. This will take a few weeks or months. Make a plan. Time it, if you can, to conclude just before the time when you think bonuses are determined. Carefully involve your supervisor but be gentle—he or she may not understand the bonus game. I'll leave it at that, but it's the old story: Set a goal, make a plan, check and control your progress, and so forth.

There are other opportunities for extraordinary pay and compensation. Some relate to special work, such as premiums directly coupled to sales performance, international assignment, and others. The other common group includes options for company stock or equivalents. This is a different game, but there are similarities. Poke around carefully and learn just what the rules of the game are: Define your goal, make your plan, and so forth.

MAPPING YOUR PAY PATH

Pay schedules are used to manage pay in your company. Sometimes these are openly published; sometimes not. Sometimes they are partially published, for instance, telling you which job grade you are in and what its ranges of pay are.

The diagrams of pay structure are not published but they are fairly simple to make. They provide insights not as easily visualized on the pay schedules unless you do a lot of calculation.

Either of them offers a map on which you can lay out the route you wish to follow with your pay growth. Let's use as an example an engineer, two years out of college, currently earning $2310 per month. Tentatively, his goal is to grow to Engineering Supervisor status eight years from now. Use the same data illustrated previously as current, but extend them to cover the Engineering Supervisor job:

	Grade			
Engineering supervisor	S8	$3510	$4380	$5250
Senior engineer	S6	$2900	$3620	$4350
Engineer	S4	$2400	$3000	$3600
Junior engineer	S2	$1980	$2480	$2970

Assume our engineer, presently just below the midpoint of job grade S2, aims to grow to mid-low job grade S8 in eight years. This pays about $3900 per month on present pay schedules. This would be an average increase of 6.5 percent per year in real-pay. But note the effect of inflation. If the illustrated 6 percent average inflation occurs, the pay schedules in eight years will be:

	Grade			
Engineering supervisor	S8	$5600	$7000	$8400
Senior engineer	S6	$4630	$5790	$6940

His inflated dollar goal at that time will be about $6200 per month. But our engineer sets his job growth milestones in terms of specific job assignments and job grades. His path is clear: his goal is to earn pay in the mid-low range of job grade S8 eight years from now. In terms of dollar raises—not real-pay—he is projecting average raises of 12 to 13 percent for these years—an ambitious goal to sustain.

PAY RAISES AND PERFORMANCE REVIEWS

The processes of personal evaluation, pay setting, and performance review differ widely from company to company. The differences are equally great among supervisors in the same company. Regardless of policy, practices of pay raises and performance reviews actually range from superb to abominable. While I have seen pockets of pay distortion and inequity, I have seen only a few. I cannot be equally charitable toward the many supervisors who fail to join the personal planning and motivation of those who work for them. For the people I have supervised, I have never experienced inequities which I was not allowed to correct in a reasonable time.

Companies budget pay and pay increases in manners similar to the processes you use to allocate your personal money. When they identify inequities or errors of pay, they try to correct those first. If they identify problems of pay, actual or anticipated, they assign a priority to preventing or correcting them. Then they balance judgments of productivity and competitive pay, based on surveys, and decide amounts of pay increases that they feel are needed. Combining all of these determines what companies want to pay.

Companies evaluate prices, product costs, and competition and decide whether they can afford the pay needs identified. With these judgments, they create a budgeted pay increase. Concurrent with this decision, companies decide whether the increases of pay represent a need to adjust schedules or whether they represent merit increases within present schedules. If needed, they prepare new schedules.

Next, instructions are prepared for the review. These include a schedule. Different instructions may be needed to respond to local problems. If the pay discipline has been good, instructions to all will be very similar. Generally, each supervisor passes the instructions to his or her lower levels. Supervisors responsible for hiring and discipline are also responsible for performance review and pay recommendations. When lower supervisors such as lead workers are used, they are required to participate in reviews.

I have observed, read about, participated in, and analyzed the processes of pay for many years. The ones I have participated in have been eminently fair. Although I have worked where criteria other than personal merit are used, I will describe only the processes of merit systems.

Systems are expressed in many ways, but I am convinced that three factors dominate all considerations in setting pay:

> *Potential Contribution.* When you are hired, your supervisor sets your pay based on judgment of the future value of your work contribution. Your judged potential when hired continues to be a factor in your pay for many years.

> *Value of Work Contribution.* This is the obvious major basis of setting all pay and is essential to the ability of a company to compete in markets for its products and in markets for good people.

> *Demonstrated Reliability and Loyalty.* After a few years, the company knows how much it can depend on you. That becomes a small but important factor in your value to your company. The company considers it in later career years.

The first and third factors contradict the equal-pay-for-equal-work concept, and I believe fairly so. Pay for potential value is a dangerous but essential effort to motivate you and entice you to stay with a company and develop. When your company judges that you are working at your potential, this pay factor falls to zero. At that time, the minor factor of reliability replaces some of the reduction. This last factor is closely related to longevity.

The weightings of the factors change throughout your career. Here is a rough approximation of their development:

	First Years 1 to 20		Middle Years 10 to 30		Late Years 25 to 40	
Potential	0.30	0.05	0.10	0.10	0.10	0.00
Work contribution	0.70	0.90	0.90	0.85	0.85	0.90
Reliability	0.00	0.05	0.00	0.05	0.05	0.10

COMPARISON

The surest way to create and sustain inequitable pay is to spread the budgeted increase evenly among all people. The second way is to give equal increases to people in the same pay grade, increasing raises to higher levels. Most companies using merit pay use controls to prevent these things from happening.

Comparison and ranking of individual contributions is the most common first step for equitable, periodic pay adjustments. This has been an informal practice of good supervisors for years. Recently, it is being formalized and improved by extending its scope.

The way it works is that employees' names are stacked in ascending position solely based on the value of their work contributions. No notation of pay or job grade is used. When people are regarded as having equal merit, the tie is broken by answering the question, "Faced with a layoff, which one would you terminate first?"

After ranking, present pay rates are added, usually in both dollars and on a graph. Exceptions—people having pay higher or lower than the general trend line—immediately stand out. Reasons for these exceptions are discussed. Emphasis is usually on how to motivate improvement those people whose pay is too high relative to recent contribution. Then initial distribution of the group's budgeted pay raises is made. Inequities are compensated to the degree that policy and consideration allow. Some may be corrected only partially. For example, a moderate raise may be given to a person whose pay is already too high, as part of a plan to motivate that person. Part of a very high raise may be held back to see if that star continues to shine. In such a case, a tentative additional raise may be planned for the near future.

Supervisors usually apply this ranking process to their own people. It may be extended by combination into larger groups. But the rating supervisor is responsible both for equity within his or her own group and maintaining the equity of the group as it is combined into higher levels. Since supervisors must discuss raises with their workers, they will try hard to make them fair. There are many cases where this comprehensive ranking produces higher individual rates than were originally proposed.

I have described merit review from the isolated viewpoint of maintaining fair pay. Pay goes hand in hand with evaluating merit in work. More important are the supervisor's expectations and plan for each of his or her workers that precedes the setting of pay. It is common to assign priority to this part of the review process. For some, it is done separately before the revision of pay rates. Understanding the pay system in your company, and your supervisor's style in giving you raises, is a key part of your career plan.

12

Pay of a Lifetime

In just a few minutes you can calculate your total pay of a lifetime for the career path you've chosen. More important, you can change your path to greatly increased work satisfaction and pay with only a little calculation and planning.

THREE CAREER PATHS

Follow me through three career paths for a whole career of pay. The odds are that you are probably on the lower of these paths. Since we will make continual reference to all three paths, I will assign them names:

Track 1. Average. If you choose to be average (over 90 percent do) you will earn at your peak a little less than twice as much real-pay as you earned in your first year of career work. (Remember that "Real-pay" is pay adjusted for inflation.) If you are on this path, your total pay for your whole career will equal 75 years of your real-pay for your first year.

Track 2. Managed Career. These people have the same potential as Average, but they dedicate 2 percent of their work time — on or off the job — to managing their careers. They have career goals, they have a real plan, they measure their achievement, and they act to stay on their plan. They work smarter, but not harder, than Average. If you advance to this path, your total pay for your whole career will increase to 100 years of your real-pay for your first year.

Track 3. Ambitious. This is the career path of people who work smarter *and* harder. Many people who move up from Track 1 to Track 2 are so pleased with their achievement that they elect to move up to Track 3. Their salary for their whole career is equal to about 150 years of their real pay for their first year, but bonuses and extra goodies increase their total career pay even more.

WHICH PATH?

You may expect me to urge you to set your goal to the Ambitious path or even higher. Nothing of the kind! What I do urge is that you know the path that you're on, and that you travel that path by deliberate decision.

Average isn't bad in a good company, but don't be average and not know it. My present subject is pay, but your decisions on pay must be woven into your decisions for your work goals.

Now and then you see some malarkey in the newspapers comparing pay differences for two career paths — college gradutes versus other people. Vague recollections are that the difference in pay for a lifetime of work used to be about $200,000 and has grown lately to well over a half-million dollars. These figures are nonsense because, for a forty- to forty-five-year career, your last year's dollars are worth only 10 percent of your first year's dollars. The nonsense of that numbers game can be overcome by using factors that represent real-pay.

PICTURES OF CAREER PAY

Figure 12.1 illustrates the inflation game as it relates to the average career. In the later years, inflation is so great that it dwarfs the differences in real-pay pictured on the same scale.

I am using these factors a little differently from the Pay Opportunity Model in Chapter 10. In this case, the factor represents the

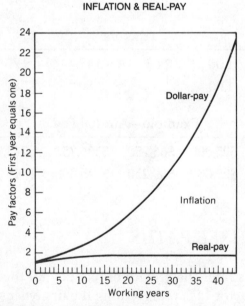

FIGURE 12.1. The inflation game—average career.

pay of your first year of work. It could be any starting pay in any year. If you're a high school graduate, it could be $8,000 or $10,000 starting pay. If you're an engineer with a master's degree, it could be $25,000 or $30,000. The dollars example at the bottom of Figure 12.1 is based on a starting pay of $1800 per month.

Look at the inflation in the last years of work. If you're only a few years into your career as you read this, by the time you retire your inflated dollar-pay can easily reach $250,000 to $300,000 per year. Sounds ridiculous, but these end-of-career factors are similar to those of people retiring currently. Because inflated dollar-pay is such a gross mask over real pay, I will base most of my discussion on real-pay. If you wish, you may apply to the values a 6 percent cumulative inflation or use the inflation factors in Figure 12.1.

	Working Years				
Work years	1	10	20	30	45
			Factors		
Dollar-pay	1.00	2.65	5.45	9.75	23.00
Real-pay	1.00	1.57	1.80	1.80	1.75
		Example – Annual Pay			
Dollar-pay	$25,000	$66,250	$136,250	$243,750	$575,000
Real-pay	$25,000	$39,250	$ 45,000	$ 45,000	$ 43,750

PAY FOR THREE PATHS

Figure 12.2 illustrates the growth of real-pay for the three careers. All start with factor 1.00, representing the first year's pay. Remember that these can be quite different dollars. The actual starting

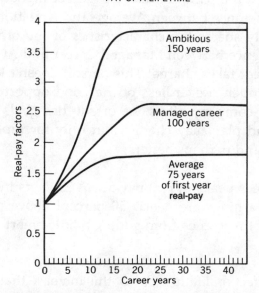

FIGURE 12.2. *Total pay for a lifetime of work expressed as years of real-pay earned in the first year.*

dollars on the Ambitious path could be lower than the starting dollars for Managed Career or Average paths. Also, someone starting on the Average path at $2000 per month could peak out at lower pay than someone starting a Managed Career at $1600 per month.

Average peaks twenty years into his or her career at 80 percent more than his or her real starting pay. After a few more years, Average's raises are smaller than the 6 percent average inflation. By the time Average retires, his or her real-pay has declined to only about 75 percent more than the pay of the first year.

Ambitious follows a career path comparable to the limit of normal ambition in the Pay Opportunity Model. That person reaches a real-pay factor of 3.6 after 15 years, but has momentum and continues to increase real earnings 25 years into his or her career.

I have sketched the path of Managed Career higher by less than half of the difference between Average and Ambitious. Managed Career partially shares the characteristics of the other two. The one key difference between Managed Career and Average is that Managed Career takes charge! This person doesn't let his or her career just happen. Regardless of the good opportunities Managed Career's company offers, he or she has goals and a plan. Both goals and plan may change, but only for replacements at least as good and perhaps better.

Managed Career peaks in real-pay about 25 years into his or her career. Peak earnings are nearly 50 percent above peak pay for Average—and this comes from adding a little smart to his or her career.

What is the effect on lifetime pay of this increase that I say results from so little effort? How much difference is there between the real lifetime earnings of these three paths?

THE DIFFERENCE—TWENTY-FIVE YEARS OF EXTRA PAY!

The total earnings of all the years for each of the three paths is easy to calculate. Then the differences become obvious.

Remember the meaning of the numbers. The factor for each year expresses the real-pay for that year as a multiple of the real earnings for the first year of the career. At peak, the factor for Managed Career is 2.65. At that time, 2.65 times the real-pay of the first working year will be earned. If Managed Career started at $10,000, real-pay at peak will be $26,500. Dollar-pay (including 25 years of inflation at 6 percent) will be more than $100,000 per year, so stick to real-pay for discussion.

Here are the total lifetime real earnings from salary. Notice the differences.

Average career   75 times first-year earnings

Managed career   100 times first-year earnings

Ambitious career   150 times first-year earnings plus other
                                     goodies!

Managed Career earns nearly 35 percent more than Average in a 40-year-plus career. Ambitious earns about 50 percent more salary than Managed Career in a total working life.

There is an additional difference for Ambitious: He or she pays a significantly higher career price than the others. Certainly money cannot be the sole motivation for increased contribution. But it is a major motivator. Ambitious's salary difference is usually supplemented by at least an equal amount of other sweeteners. These differ among companies. A series of incentive bonuses compensate Ambitious directly and currently for extraordinary contributions. Stock options, or equivalents, provide additional compensation but are dependent on performance of the whole company, and on performance of the price of its stock in the market.

Combining both salary difference and performance premiums, Ambitious earns well over 150 times the first-year real-pay in his or her whole career. This is more than twice the lifetime real earnings of Average.

NO IVORY TOWER, NO LOFTY PEAKS

Don't forget that I have illustrated career paths achievable by many people. None of this urges vice-presidential goals. At the highest, Ambitious will only nudge the lower side of the executive pay schedule. Managed Career will stay well below the highs of the salaried pay schedule. Someone starting in the hourly pay schedule will achieve the pay factors of Managed Career with only moderate penetration into the salaried schedule.

YES, BUT THE TAX BITE

Obviously, the increasing tax bite is a partial career demotivator. How bad is it? Some of the answer is apparent because few of us fail to go after more pay. Paying even 35 percent of each additional dollar for tax is discouraging.

The money side of the answer seems to lie in the concept of what the gains contribute to your disposable income—that is, what's left after taxes and the necessities (housing, food, clothing, and transportation). Even though your life-style gets more expensive as your career advances, your money options seem to get a little better; there's an attractive increase in your disposable income.

COLLEGE VERSUS NONCOLLEGE

Can we use the information on career paths to get a better understanding of this controversy? Maybe. First, recognize that the issue is dominated by factors other than money. If the richness of your life comes from other than the academic knowledge and its use, money is not the issue. If you acquire the knowledge you want by other means, particularly by on-the-job learning, money is a small part of the issue.

But money is our interest in the issue for now. Compare the two paths in terms of our information.

Assume two average careers. High School Graduate (HSG) starts at the lowest wage; Qualified College Graduate (QCG) starts at twice the low wage. Because they both travel an average path, both will have lifetime earnings equal to about seventy-five times the real-pay of their first year.

Because QCG's pay is twice as great, he or she will earn 150 times HSG's first-year pay. If QCG's field of study is a favored one— currently the technical fields—he or she will more likely earn 170 to 200 years of the starting pay of HSG. In summary, QCG will earn more than twice as much lifetime career pay.

What if QCG goes on the average track and the HSG selects the ambitious path? Then HSG, with modest luck and incentive premium pay, will earn lifetime pay approximately equal to that of QCG. Remember that the ambitious path includes the concept of working harder.

I know quite a few of these people and it usually does not work that way. When the high school graduate gets bit by the career growth bug, he or she goes for the whole deal—education and ambition! So it's back to school for the degree and it's Managed Career at the least. I know so many who take this great path. Many start late. Many resume college after having dropped out. I stand in awe of some who start at age thirty-five and slave for six years for that degree. It's a proud badge to wear!

CAN YOU AFFORD TO BE AVERAGE?

This concept of lifetime earnings, with its simple way to avoid the confusion of inflation, is a strong invitation for you to take another simple, lifetime view. In a few minutes, you can convert all of your major expenditures for your lifetime into years-of-first-year-pay. In other words, you will have the elements of a lifetime budget.

For example, look at the major expenses of a moderate middle-class life for a college graduate. Your housing (purchase, mortgage interest, utilities, maintenance, insurance, etc.) will cost you about thirty years of your first-year's pay. Your cars will cost you about ten more years to pay.

Necessities and near-necessities (food, clothing, college tuition, medical expenses, taxes, etc.) can easily add up to another forty or fifty years of pay. Obviously, this has to be a two-earner family. But even more than one income may not give the family the moderately good life that most of us have come to expect.

WHAT'S THE ANSWER?

Again, the obvious. Realize early that basic career management is the easiest way to get your share of an essentially good life. More important, it's one way to increase your personal fulfillment.

NO FREEBIES

I have repeated that there are no freebies in the career game. I wonder . . . . The difference between a Managed Career and an Average Career is almost a no-cost deal. The additional rewards, in satisfaction as well as money, are quite large.

So very little is required of you to manage your career that it's almost free. The added rewards of success—for you and your company—are completely out of proportion to the minor investment required. Almost inevitably, the added effort is shared by your company.

Besides, the managing game is a delight and satisfaction of itself. Your only risk is that you will catch the bug and have to go after at least one more level.

SECTION 3

Doing It!

13

Changing Your Field

Do you hear the call—the call to roam, the call to change your work, or even the call to change your company? They're all part of the game. Whether they come from others or from inside you, they can set you off for whole new fields. The game I'm speaking of is elective change—for whatever reason, you *want* to make a change.

Changing your field means either or both of two things:

Change the kind of work you do.

Change your company.

Do the first *carefully*; do the second *reluctantly*.

Many of you will probably change from the career path you planned before starting work. Sometimes your first change happens when you accept your first job offer. You are offered something different than you had planned and it's attractive, or you discover after you've worked awhile that the work you planned is not for you—it's not what you expected, or it doesn't satisfy you.

More often, your first work becomes a platform from which you can see jobs in the company and industry that you couldn't see before. You see attractive jobs that you didn't know about, and you understand them better because of your new work experience.

Change your work carefully, because you're still looking at only the top of the pile; there are many more jobs for you to see. Unless you make a specific effort to examine other fields, you may make a change before seeing a more attractive path.

Change your company *reluctantly* for deeper reasons. Your company is far more important to your life and career than you may recognize. Its personal importance, like ties to your family and friends, may be obscured by the attraction of challenging new fields of work, and money. You may characterize your company as being those remote, nonexistent, people I referred to before—"they." In reality, your company is more those people with whom you work and achieve.

I'm not getting ready to sing "Auld Lang Syne." Among other things, companies have to be institutions of practical, selfish fulfillment. If it is to be "your" company, if you are to have a continuing association, it will be because you work with its people toward shared goals. More than that, you must share some responsibility to shape its path. Don't change companies without a searching evaluation of both the old and the new. Make sure that the change is for real personal needs that can't be filled well in your present company.

CHANGING YOUR WORK

Your desire to change your field of work often comes in two steps. First, as you work, you learn about other jobs in your company. This spurs your interest and you talk and read about other jobs, both inside and outside of your company.

Step two develops as you realize how many job choices are available to you because of your personal ability. You get an intuitive understanding of the second theme that I keep repeating: You have personal potential beyond your previous dreams.

This ability is waiting to be called into action. Compare yourself to your peers as you learn the work. You will see a few exceptions and specialists, but you soon realize that you are on the way to being on a par with the best if you want that. You learn from them and you gain experience and practice. That's when you should commit to stretch a little and make a plan to achieve a little more, a little sooner.

There's something else that you should be doing at this time, and not many people do it. Look at the people several levels above you. Not just as groups, but as individuals who represent work at those levels. Try getting to know them or at least to know about them so that you can imagine what they were like when they occupied jobs similar to your present one.

You'll realize immediately that these people had qualifications comparable to your own when they were in work similar to your present work. Sure, they were the best people of their group at the time, but the big difference was their realization of their personal potential and their understanding—conscious or intuitive—of how the game is played.

There is a wider range of jobs available and accessible to you than you know. Your potential is as good as those who are presently performing and growing in those higher jobs. Rather than pushing you to work for the higher jobs, I am pushing you to realize your potential early, to know early that it is your choice now to decide in what path and at what level you will work. Understand now, and never look back and say, "If I had only understood then."

Your company is your means of developing and applying this potential of yours. It's not just that your company can use your potential, or that you can inject your ability into your company, it *needs* you to experience your growth and make your contribution through it. This is an invitation to decide a better course for both you and for your company. It is your decision, but your company wants to influence you.

I can't tell you whether changing your field is easy by nature or whether it becomes easy as you learn to play the game. My first deliberate change was hard and took several years. My later changes have been easier, intriguing, and satisfying.

I know that exterior events—luck, circumstances, timing, the breaks—are all factors, but you have to be ready and willing to react to them. I'm not suggesting that you jump every time you hear the bell ring, but that you anticipate and prepare for the opportunities. Even if it's not the one you wanted or anticipated, you're still ready to give it deliberate consideration.

INVITATIONS TO CHANGE

There are many situations that you should consider as invitations to change your field. A typical one is your company acquiring a new function, new technology, or new equipment. Someone must handle it; why not you? Your company needs people to get it started and to sustain it.

Management faces a choice of how to staff in these situations. If other companies are ahead of yours in the new method, your company may have to acquire people who are already experienced, or it may start with its own people or a combination of current employees and new ones. No matter how your company intends to staff such opportunities, you stand a good chance of entering this new field if you play your cards right. I've done it. I've seen it done. I know it's your chance.

An even better situation is for you to conceive the change, to sell the new process and to manage its acquisition and implementation. Whatever the case, entering early gives you an advantage and recognition as a pioneer (along with the risk of pioneering, of course).

Implied invitations to change your field are expressed in many work situations. You have to develop the habit of querying yourself, "Is there an opportunity for me in this change?" I used an example earlier of someone who regarded a support function as ineffective. When you have ideas of how to improve a service, it may be an attractive opportunity to change your field.

When you are regarded as being competent and flexible, you are likely to receive overt invitations to change your field of work. Be careful of being flattered by such an invitation; the flattery may cloud your decision and bargaining situation. Be prepared to receive the opportunity with gratitude but with reservation; take time to probe and understand the situation. It is really an opportunity for you? What are the risks? Is there a significant price to pay in your personal and family situation? Permeating all of the issues is the question of whether you have any bargaining power and if so how much.

Don't view these situations as just happening at high levels. They're whizzing by at all levels; you just haven't bothered to turn on and tune in. Remember, most of the opportunities are taken before they're announced or become public knowledge. Almost no hourly people search for or create their own opportunities. Some trust in fate. Nearly all depreciate their ability until invited and expected from above. Nearly all fail to realize that they can influence management decisions of their company as they affect their work.

DOING IT

Changing your field means changing your job. Sometimes the sequence is reversed: You spot an interesting job and decide to change to that field of work. Spotting a new type of work you want before you define and identify the job you need is tough. You will need it for your conversion and the odds are high that you will have to take an interim job as a transition.

For either case, you must convince someone to subsidize your transition. If you are in a low-level job and the change is within your company, the change may be easy. At higher levels and with major changes of fields, the change will be harder.

How about age? Although the legal prohibition against age discrimination suggests that it sometimes poses a problem, I can only offer you optimism. In all the cases I know, both personal and observed, the normal barrier is the person and not the company as far as age is concerned. If you have maintained your education and your enthusiasm, someone will take a chance with you. If you have closed your mind and your spirit, if you have turned away from your company for your growth and spirit, stick with the field that you're in.

If you need an interim step to the job that you want, most good companies will sustain your present pay in a lower job if you convince them that your change is for the common good. You can find some reasons why your present work will be of some value in the new assignment.

Acquiring knowledge for a new job is almost certainly a required key to changing your field. Having a plan to learn may convince your sponsor to invest in your change. He or she may be especially impressed if you have already started when you approach him or her. Going back to school is the obvious way and the way most people expect. It's good and has advantages, but it may not be as good as on-the-job learning. As I have said before, I'm not speaking of just rub-off from work. Good on-the-job learning means planning to acquire specific subject knowledge and tying it to real applications in work situations—backing up your work with supplementary reading and directed discussion at work.

Make your own plan; get help if you need it. Help may consist only of being able to discuss it with someone. Don't blabber or broadcast. If you are excellent in your present work, someone in another field will be complimented that you want to change to his or her field of work.

The attitude of your present supervisor to you and to your proposed change is critical to your move. Even if your change is to another company, your supervisor may be contacted. Your supervisor's attitude toward your change is composed of many things: his or her need for you on the job; his or her view of your obligation to your work and to him or her (Have you more than returned the supervisor's investment in you?); how the supervisor's manager views the situation; the supervisor's personal desire to see you advance, and so forth. Your critical decision is whether to ask for his or her help for your change. Be prepared to suggest a replacement for your job if you're asked. Make leaving in good grace a part of your plan.

Make your move! Keep a small folder with notes on your plan. For each step, make a few notes of what you expect and questions that need answers. Evaluate your results and make notes after each move.

My first request for a planned change was well received. I remember thinking after the interview, "He's enthusiastic but he won't do anything. What do I do?" I decided to wait, but I started some related education and continued to develop my plan. In a few months the organization changed. I repeated my request to the new manager and I was accepted.

That change was like many—initial conflicts between urgent needs to perform and requirements to learn the new field of work. This makes for a frantic but exciting work situation. You look back on stages of that kind and say, "I wouldn't do it again, but it was all worth the result."

What about pay? If you're changing companies, the opportunity has to be really terrific to change without an excellent raise. Inside changes rarely bring an immediate raise. I know of few firm promises of big rewards—promotion, big pay increases, or job grade changes—that come with any inside job change. I know of several cases when the principal interpreted the discussion of change as a commitment for reward or promotion. The time to confirm any such commitment is before you agree to the change, and you are the person most responsible for clarifying the conditions of the change. Make notes to yourself of these conditions. Those notes are good for only one purpose—confirming to yourself what you expected when you made the change.

You may think it sounds like I'm preparing you to expect broken promises on changes. Quite the opposite! Nearly all of the changes I've seen had good results. The few that turned sour seemed to have had flaws or misunderstandings from the start.

When you've made your plans and your decision, you may have moments of hesitancy; most people do. In my first change, I was promoted to my boss's job two years after the change. He was easy to talk with, and I discussed my concern with following in his footsteps. He said, "Not only will you do well, you will experience a revolution in your pay." His words were more than simply reassurance; they were his expectation of me. He was right; the change paid off in both job satisfaction and pay.

STAY WITH THE PROFESSION?

If your education or commitment is to professional work, the idea of changing your field can upset you. You feel like you're abandoning your old ties and security.

There is a simple test you can make of the strength of your ties. It rests on part of the definition of the word "profession." A profession involves work associated with a recognized body of complex knowledge. Part of the responsibility of professional work is extending the knowledge or extending its application. Regardless of how you do it or how you communicate it, it's part of belonging to the profession.

It only takes a few years to know whether you're in the right profession. Are you really pushing to expand the knowledge and its application? When your answer is No, you should be able to leave and go on to other work without feeling any pull. Your knowledge, your contacts, and your experience are often good background for your new work. Once again, early recognition that you have a problem and considered action are the best solution.

PIED PIPERS—THE ENTICERS

Oh, hear the recruiters' pipes! By long distance telephone, by letters, papers, and magazines, they woo you:

> Face it, dum dum, you will never manage your own career. Examine this goodie I offer you, a prefabricated career plan. I will personally transport you to a land of milk and honey, the land of sugarplum trees. Just your first reward will be a 25 to 50 percent pay raise. And the work! Ah, you will work at the leading edge of your field, where you belong!

It's partly true—if you can't or don't develop your own career and take care of yourself in your company, the recruiter may do it better than you will ever do it for yourself.

Tick off the issues involved in this appeal. The most important is, "Will I ever do for myself in my company what this change might do for me in the new company?"

How long will you really keep the pay differential? Will you like the new company—not "The Company," but the work you will do and the people you will work with? How about the location? And where will you stand if the company turns sour? Can you replace your current insurance and pension plans without loss of benefits? How will the family take the change?

But one issue persists regardless of whether you change: *Will you manage your career?* Will you develop personal attachment to the company so that it becomes "your" company?

THE ONE EXCEPTION

Since page one I have emphasized, "Stick with your company, learn how to use it." I recognize one obvious exception to that advice. If your company or your supervisor enforces scheduled, nonmerit advancement, then move. Move yourself to where the value of your work determines your progress, in opportunity and pay.

I am not speaking of some introductory or probationary job phase. Various companies or work situations may insist on an initial, scheduled entry to the company or an assignment. Also, I recognize the value of phased work introductions extending from a few weeks to several years. These can be valuable, but the bad ones can be little better than indentured slavery, which require paying a personal price for opportunity. The same effect results from the personal whim of a supervisor who insists that everyone serve two years in some menial task to be eligible for promotion.

Move away from these situations. If the problem is your supervisor, carefully ask for an enlarged assignment. If you get the routine formula response, move. If it permeates your company, written policy or not, test the policy with a quiet try. Observe whether the policy is rigidly applied. If it is, move.

THE ONE FIRM ACTION—AND IT'S WRONG!

There are many people whose single positive act of career management is to change companies. Most of these people are reluctant to face their supervisor or some other member of their company and say, "I want a change."

Further, they view an invitation from another company as a prefabricated solution to their career problems, which they haven't bothered to define. They do outside what they won't do inside their company. They define goals: "Leave my company and get a higher paying, better opportunity in another company." They make a plan: "Define the tasks, the milestones, the schedule, and the resources to make it happen." They stop worrying about the people less capable than they who are doing better than them, but they are heading for that same situation in a new company in a few months unless they identify and solve their basic problem.

What's wrong? Most often it's a shared failure of the person and his or her company. Here's an illustration.

A young man in a staff administrative job had worked in a small, technological company for several years. He volunteered to me with pride his record of growth and pay. Then he was attracted by a newspaper advertisement offering challenging work and a 25 percent pay raise. (I call it the "Standard Offer Of Challenging Work and 25 percent Pay Raise.")

When he left, his supervisor urged him to stay and offered an attractive raise. Then an executive upped the ante to a 35 percent raise, a little more than what he was getting to move—but his commitment had been made.

This was a failure of both person and company. Either or both could have kept the man in a better career situation than the one to which he moved. Both should have been adjusting shared goals and needs.

14

Using Your Supervisor

Your key to career growth, personal development, and excellent pay is a series of increasingly challenging work assignments. To get those essential opportunities you need to learn how to use your supervisor.

This does not imply trying to dominate him or her, nor taking the best work from others. But it may require changing your supervisor's thinking, and yours, about any person's right and expectation of sharing work opportunities in your company.

For example, it is a widely accepted practice for supervisors to assign work to the person most capable of doing it well. This is wrong. If all people are expected to develop, be it a necessity or a right, then some fraction of all the work must be used for training and personal growth. Fortunately, this is best for both the people, and the company—and the supervisor.

In addition to setting aside a small fraction of all tasks as a medium of learning, the supervisor must regard each of his or her people as needing to work in certain tasks to develop new skills and knowledge, or to refresh and maintain those skills. Regardless of how your supervisor views his or her job and you, you want to get your supervisor to assign you the series of job tasks that you need to learn and grow.

Understanding your supervisor's job, and recognizing different perspectives from which people view supervision, will give you a special entry to all of the work opportunities that the supervisor can make available to you. You may be able to understand the foundation of your supervisor's job better than your supervisor does.

This chapter will cover three areas:

Understanding your supervisor's job.

Considering some cases, good and bad.

Taking action: What do you do? How do you do it? How fast?

YOUR SUPERVISOR'S JOB

In the press of the day's work, the basic patterns of your supervisor's work may not be apparent. Many supervisors, good or bad, may not recognize or use these patterns. After you have read this brief description of this vital work, challenge the concepts. Then watch for a few days and associate what you see with these ideas.

Supervision of people working in a business company has two main facets:

Managing the work

Developing the people

Despite all the baloney poured forth in innumerable seminars and training courses, these two facets make up what's vital in the flow of your supervisor's work. A third primary facet, administration, fills out your boss's day. Administration may be the greatest user of his or her time. This is okay, and frequently necessary, so long as it doesn't squeeze out the vital two.

Next, let's consider each of these two facets in more depth. It is obvious that types of work are so dissimilar that I can't create a basic picture that you can use to understand all work. But if you can discern the fundamentals, you have a major tool for managing your career.

Managing Work

Now we're back to the same management system that I've suggested you use to manage your career. The three steps again:

Set work goals

Make a plan

Control the work

Actually, another step belongs between "make a plan" and "control the work"—execution. Execution is actually doing the work you're managing; it's closely related but not a part of the management system as such.

No matter how tough and confused your work situation gets, this is the framework on which to manage it. When you're trying to sort things out and make sense of confusion, use this framework.

To understand each of the three basic steps of managing work look briefly at each activity that makes up your supervisor's work management system. Assume for this exercise that your supervisor is doing all the work management alone, doing so will help you understand the supervisor's job, even though what I will urge is that you do some of the job for your supervisor.

You want to participate in supervisory work; that is, by some means compatible with your supervisor's style and with your style, you want to assume some of the responsibility for managing your work. That may not be easy. Some supervisors want to retain that responsibility for themselves. Some will resent your trying to assume any of that task. Fortunately, others may be receptive to your trying, even proud of having you grow to that kind of responsibility. At the least, you want to learn and understand the work management system; at most, with your supervisor's concurrence, you can start your first steps to actual participation in management.

Work Goals. Clearly defined work goals are necessary for people to do effective work. Many people who work ineffectively do so primarily because they have no clear picture of what is expected of them. This primary use of work goals, then, is to communicate and verify that people know what they are expected to do.

The second need for goals is almost magic. People with clear work goals do more work, particularly people who are invited to participate in setting their own goals and the goals of their work team. How much more? Would you believe twice as much? It's true. Improvements of 25 to 50 percent are common, and twice as much is not rare.

Setting work goals is one tough part of your supervisor's job. Your supervisor commits to management for the group's goal achievement and, in turn, wants you to commit and achieve your goal. When you volunteer for a challenging performance, you take a real burden from your supervisor.

Work Plans. Mention planning and most people think of the "what, who, when, how" of achievement. That's proper, but the exciting approach to planning is to realize that the supervisor is building a model. He or she has the freedom and opportunity to create a work model, using his or her resources and shaping the parameters. A supervisor's work model for his or her group is a collage of tactics, schemes, problems, and solutions. And, into this model of work the supervisor weaves deliberate development of his or her people.

Execution. Making it happen is the essence of the work that is so richly varied from supervisor to supervisor and work group to work group. Execution is made up of the elements that you lay on your system's framework to create your understanding of work and opportunity.

Control. This is the least recognized, least understood, and most often forgotten part of managing work. A simple explanation helps: Persons or groups are in control when they do what they committed to do. Note that this implies having a goal and a plan. No plan, no control.

Consider two kinds of uncontrolled work, one fairly good, the other very poor. The better is done by the committed person, the one who comes to work each day committed to do "the best I can." The approach used is based on a poor foundation—"No one can do better than his best." But you do good work, alone or as a group, when you understand your work, have a goal, and have a plan to achieve it.

"Best-you-can" achieves only average at best. You do good, competitive work when you commit to goals and plans. Committing to goals makes for pegpoints of achievement that help you overcome the petty obstacles that arise every day. When you plan, you anticipate these problems and discover new opportunities in time to do something about them.

The other uncontrolled work is uncommitted. It is generally done by good people who are willing and waiting for direction but are not committed. The basis of control is pausing regularly to evaluate and model your near future: What are you going to achieve if you keep going like you're going? What correction, change, or improvement do you need to stay on track, or schedule? This is exactly like controlling your car—scanning the road to anticipate, avoid, or solve your problems, and to confirm that you're on the right course.

Developing People

Supervisors develop their people when they assist them to do more challenging work or to add new work skills. Their medium of doing this is the work itself. Working in tasks that require higher skills or different skills is the primary means of developing and growing.

You must have a minimum share of these assignments simply to avoid career obsolescence. You must have more than a minimum of these assignments to accomplish your career growth. Your supervisor is your primary source of opportunity for this kind of development, but the initiative for your growth can be either yours or your supervisor's. The optimum is that both of you share initiative for your growth. Nothing can fully replace work assignments as your means of career development.

How about education and training courses? They are great means of acquiring new knowledge. Some instructors and some courses, provide practice or near-practice in their teaching that approach the real thing. Training tends to emphasize knowledge regarding a particular kind of work. Generally, education aims to be broader, to develop the whole person, with less emphasis on a particular type of work.

But using the work itself for acquiring new knowledge combines the best of both of these worlds. Your supervisor is in an excellent position to impart knowledge of today's work. And if you've caught your supervisor's enthusiasm, you'll be eager to acquire this knowledge. But you must supply more of the energy to use the present work for broader understanding—education—that supplies the solid foundation you need for your future.

The Big Obstacle. Why do people not develop, or slow down in their development? Because of one big obstacle: the powerful combination of a supervisor's prejudice and the person's self-image. They are a single obstacle because they combine in relentless synergy.

This prejudice is not of race, religion, sex, or handicap, so widely discussed these days. Rather it is that someone looks at you, or works briefly with you, and immediately assumes what your work potential is. And you look at yourself and mistake simple inexperience and ignorance for inability. With these twin blunders of judgment, so common that they are nearly the norm, the tremendous potential that you, and most people, have for growth is masked.

There is no way of determining the excellent work of which you are capable without giving you an opportunity to do that work, being ready to coach you if you ask for it, and providing the expectation of your succeeding.

Why are learning and growing *in the work* so good? Because they give you immediate confirmation of their value, and at the same time you have confirmation that you can do it. This kind of joint performance is the essence of the bonds between persons and company.

Your Supervisor's Priorities. How high does your personal development rank among your supervisor's priorities? Stack the requirements and pressures with which supervisors contend and see:

Today's work

Today's administration

Managing tomorrow's work

Developing people

Your supervisor sincerely wants—needs—you to develop. But left alone he or she has to set a low priority on your development. You see, we've written a choice for you into the equation; you cannot afford to leave your supervisor alone. At the same time, however, you can intercede for yourself in a manner that can be very helpful to your supervisor. Your approach must satisfy common needs.

CASES

The easiest situation for you is when your supervisor takes the initiative to develop you, or encourages your initiative to develop yourself. The worst situation is when your supervisor overtly opposes your efforts. In between these are the passive cases when your boss doesn't help or hinder—you're on your own. This last doesn't sound good, but you can use your initiative to make out well on a do-it-yourself basis.

Opposition

Mark is a mechanic's helper two years out of high school. He's young and impatient, but he knows it. He didn't like school and didn't get along well with his teachers. He's committed to "makin' it" and knows he has to make it with his work.

Mark is a realist. He has good native intelligence. He understands himself and his career situation. His impatience is giving him a hard time. Working in a big maintenance organization, he realizes that the people on the job represent alternatives that he can let his career take. They range from his boss's boss who made it the hard way, to fellows who have been working thirty years and are only one job grade ahead of him.

The idea of deliberate career success is Mark's kind of thing. Setting and achieving goals is intuitive for him. He accepted immediately that seeking challenging task assignments was a good way for him to learn and grow quickly. Seeing this as a tactic, one that he has made work, is a satisfaction to him. He foresaw his supervisor as a problem rather than an aid. He solved it by avoiding it. When he could spare a few minutes, he attached himself to people or groups using skills or doing tasks that he needed to learn and to be accepted as knowing how to do.

Mark's approach involved three decisions that matched his style, his needs, and the attitudes of people with whom he worked.

First, he assisted others on his own, rather than ask his supervisor or the other workers. He believed his supervisor would deny him the opportunities.

Second, he attached himself to others' work rather than ask if they wanted his help. This felt more natural to him; it was his personal style. He joined their work; he didn't mind doing the menial parts of the work; he didn't resent the comments—"eager-beaver" and so forth—that resulted from his extra work.

Third, he recognized that people's *perception* of him as having the skills, and having enthusiasm in his work, was nearly as important as the skills and experience as such.

But then Mark blew it! He knew immediately that he had blown his cork once more. Mark spotted an operation being planned that he wanted to work on; it was an experience that he needed. It was remote; he had no chance of simply attaching himself to the work. So, he asked his supervisor for assignment to the job. His supervisor refused and made a remark about Mark's working without assignment. The request was an obvious trigger; both people let loose the differences they had been building. Surely this sounds familiar. It's the immature reactions we all have when differences build between people.

Consider, as Mark did, how he could make positive use of this and similar problems, not just to recover, but as an experience of lasting value. What did he do wrong? Are there some things that he did right? Better still, what approach could he use next time to continue the string of successes that he had going?

Generally, no single event, no matter how bad, will destroy a valuable, ongoing relationship. Blowups blow over. Apologize early and let it die. Don't aggravate the problem by extended discussion.

The Emperor and the Court Jester

Using your supervisor implies a one-way street. But it's not; it can equally benefit the supervisor being used.

The Emperor and the Court Jester is just such a case, one in which both got immense benefits from a very close personal relationship in their company, and their relationship brought immense satisfaction and benefits to other people in the company.

I worked with these two people when they were both late into their relationship. My understanding is a combination of first hand information and fill-ins.

The Emperor was a genius of business management. Like a Michelangelo, his business interests covered the whole gamut of the business—create, make, market, and support functions. Along with all of his knowledge and comprehensive perspective, he was endowed with enthusiastic drive to make it go and compassion that drew the support of the people that he needed.

The Jester was harder to characterize. Older than his chief, he had grown up with a less-refined background, and he was proud of it. He had gleaned a wealth of practical knowledge from his life experience, a mixture of understanding people and the tough aspects of business. His approach was rough and blunderous.

These two were joined by a close personal relationship, almost like dear brothers; each needed and used the other. Through several career stretches, their attachment strengthened. Their mutual attraction was hard to define, but one element of it was the Jester's sense of humor. While he overstepped the bounds of propriety occasionally, his wisecracks broke the tension of many an executive impasse. A flip remark from his tough background made many a failure tolerable. His relief of the frequent tensions was a valuable, essential contribution.

And in return his supervisor, the Emperor, carried this man to the executive levels, to personal wealth and acceptance in executive circles. While some of his independent operations could be challenged, his continued association with the Emperor made the contribution of this very average person a real substitute for excellence.

ACTION

You're ready to act. You have in mind the basics of your supervisor's job. This a well-considered, low-keyed program. At the same time, you sustain controlled impatience and commitment to interact with your supervisor, on the job, to grow in the work and skills and to grow in your pay.

The one theme that is pervasive to your development program that you want to share with your supervisor is "Try Me." Put any problems and obstacles aside initially. (This is the reverse of much advice. You often hear, "Well, if you can't solve the problems, all of your plans and efforts are wasted," and similar pessimism. It's the wrong approach.)

Decide first what you're reaching for. What do you want? The first thing is nearly always the goal. Again, this is the really tough part, since combinations of people and situations are so different. Keep the "Supervisor, Try Me" approach in mind as you consider a common problem situation.

You are forty years old and, looking back, realize that you've "topped out." Your assignments are less challenging and your pay increases are poor. You recognize that the challenging work, and the pay, are going to others, usually younger people. You're too young to be old. Your performance reviews are okay, but they don't express much expectation on either side. Face it; you and your company have let your career get into the doldrums.

What action do you take? *You* decide what you want. Set your goal and make your plan. *Then* ask your supervisor to help—"Try me."

Develop How Fast?

The second common misconception about personal development is that it takes a long time. You can develop much faster than you generally realize. There are few jobs in all of industry of which you can't be fully capable in twelve to eighteen months.

What's the obstacle then? Simple—embedded attitudes. "It has always been this way." You're expected to soak in the job three to five years to get the experience and learning. After all, that's what your supervisor was made to do; there must be some reason for the tradition. Besides, if you learn it in fifteen months, it implies that the job is not as valuable as presently thought.

There are cases where this kind of thinking is expressed very bluntly. I have heard that it is not unusual for master mechanics to hide their layout work from other mechanics to prevent their learning too fast, and threatening their own jobs.

"Be patient. There'll be plenty of chances later for you to learn." This kind of response may be valid; you may not be ready for the challenge you're asking, or someone else may deserve it more. But most often the reluctance to assign you a challenge is part of the "we've-always-done-it-this-way" thinking.

How fast can you expect to develop? Flip back to Figure 8.2. It's a good picture comparing alternate approaches. Consider the lower curve as representing average growth for a person who accepts the conventional. The top curve represents only a deliberate approach by an average person, someone who makes his or her job moves happen by going after specific assignments.

Is that the whole story? Not at all. I said the times are for an average person; if you're in a hurry, if you need to grow faster, you can. You must be careful, but you can make your supervisor a prime resource for your career management. Remember that using your supervisor fills common needs—yours and the supervisor's. Don't hesitate to shape your supervisor's contribution to your career.

15

Here's How!

Now it's time to pull all of the concepts together, to create your action plan, to execute it! Start by summarizing two basic patterns which you are preparing to use.

First is the specific pattern of career management, made up of two cycles which you will repeat five or ten times in the first half of your career:

Get a new, better job

Suceed—perform effectively—in that job

The second pattern is the management system, the fundamental process used to manage major achievement. Call this by other names—the goal-seeking system, success management, whatever you please—but it's the same basic process. The "how" of career management is the sum of all the "hows" of applying the three basic elements of management itself:

How do you develop *goals*?

How do you make a *plan*?

How do you *control*?

And these cluster around the main element:

How do you *execute*?

This same pattern applies to both of the two career cycles: getting a new job and succeeding in the job. Your resources are different and you use different tactics, but the same pattern applies: set goals, make a plan, and control.

There's a magic in the process, but there's no secret to it. Many achievers reinvent it for themselves. Some lucky people use it intuitively. Whether or not they express it in these words, they recognize it as their system. It's learnable. The only decision you have to make is whether you want to discipline and control yourself to achieve increased career satisfaction.

Recognize that by taking *any* action whatever you are considering becoming different—different from what you have been, different from others.

Many of you want to launch your career management by starting with a new job. That's okay. When you develop your new job goals and your plan, you will realize that improving your control over and contribution to your present job is the beginning of your new job goal, the starting point of managing your career.

GOALS

Developing goals is the first and toughest part of the system you're learning how to use. It doesn't get easier. As you achieve the near-term goals, developing and stretching to new longer range goals is nearly as hard as developing your original ones.

Don't start with the idea that you're searching for the one good goal ordained for you. There are many good goals available for you, a variety of good work in which you can succeed. The important first step is: Exercise your career management ability and experience a success as a result of your personal effort.

Recognize the three parts of your goal-setting task:

1. Setting your work goal is your primary task. Begin by selecting your field of work, then the part of your company in which you want to work next. After that, select the jobs that you want and decide when you want them. For example, "My new job goal is to manage all professional recruiting—for manufacturing, engineering, and management—by June, four years from now."

2. Next, set your pay goal. It is second in importance to your work goal. At the least, it measures the growth in *value* you plan for your work. For example, "My pay goal is to advance my job grade and pay from my present position in job grade S2 to a similar position in job grade S6." This will mean an average real-pay raise of about 10 percent per year. That's a tough goal and may be too high to be realistic. Remember, real pay is before you add inflation.

3. Resource goals come later. After you develop your plan, test each activity to verify that you have or can get the resources to achieve it. The "can gets," such as new knowledge, experience, and assistance, become the resource goals necessary to support your work goals. For example, "I can probably achieve my job goal without additional formal education, by on-the-job learning. But later, if I want to become Personnel Manager, I will need and be expected to have a masters degree in business administration or administrative science. So, I set my goal on an MBA degree in June, three years from now."

Work Goal

Reduced to basics, how do you identify the job you want and set a schedule to achieve it?

Search the functions of your company for work that looks interesting and attractive. Generally, look up two or three levels above your present work, but don't worry too much about the level.

Ignore your present job and pay, your education and experience, and your present job knowledge. Similarly, ignore the barriers that you think may lie between you and those potential job goals. Two common ones are "Who's the competition?" and "Will there be an opening when I need it?"

Select the most attractive of these jobs that you want. Simple? Not really. If you know your company and work area even fairly well, and many people do, it may be simple. I'm going to suggest a way to do it that will assure you that you've covered the territory.

Consider all work of business and industry as being composed of just four types:

Create, Make, Market. These are the three primary types of work that are directly associated with designing, producing, and selling products and services.

Services and Support. This fourth group includes many types of work not directly related to products but necessary for primary work to be done. This work includes Personnel, data processing, purchasing, control, finance, legal, maintenance, and several others.

Regardless of what your company does, it has some mix of these kinds of work. If you search for your job goal using them as a guide, you will have covered the whole territory. For example, a hamburger restaurant is largely making and selling work, but you can define its jobs on this framework. A legal partnership has all of its work bunched in services and support, but you can understand its work array with this approach.

More important, the same approach allows you to organize your understanding of work in a large, diverse company such as a high-technology manufacturing company. You can use this approach to evaluate your whole company or for evaluating the jobs in a small section in which you are interested.

Once you've surveyed your company and the work you want on this basis, you can decide whether you want to select a job goal in one or more of these work areas. Give serious consideration to all areas that exist in your company, without regard to your present experience and skills.

How do you survey the work areas of your company in this framework if you have only limited knowledge of your company? You must learn about your company. You may limit your initial search to whatever small area that you know about; that still may offer a large variety of opportunity. But later you will need to expand your knowledge of your company's work.

Going deeper, how do you get to know more about your company? The prime way is to talk to people. Go out of your way to talk to people about their work. Regardless of what other methods you use, this is the best.

What are the other methods? Read published information, but don't worry if you don't understand all of what you read. Read your company's annual reports and employee publications, as well as newspaper articles about the company, and the company's recruiting advertisements. Carefully use unrestricted internal documents such as organization charts, information on bulletin boards, and even telephone directories. Read with extra care the information that comes to you about your job. All of these sources have more information than you have been trying to use in the past. You may find that careful questioning will get you more than you expect. Don't forget the obvious: Carefully ask your supervisor or someone in Personnel if there is a list of jobs and their descriptions that you can use. Even if your request is refused, it's a reasonable one.

SCHEDULING AND PRIORITIES

Although I have suggested specifics of how to manage your career, I am sure you recognize, as I do, that these depend on your personal style, just as your goals depend on your personal values.

However, I don't think you can take the same latitude with your schedule. Experience convinces me that you must make steady progress in your initial planning cycle or you will bog down.

Don't lose sight of fundamentals: you are developing a job goal as your first step of career management. This may be a major change for you, a tough test. It may be your first step toward self-reliance in your career. If you are apprehensive (this is normal), you will be tempted to look for excuses to postpone and stretch the process. Don't do it!

This is your first need for control. How you do it is simple: Set a date for completion. I repeat my earlier advice: Schedule six weeks on your calendar by which to complete your first job goals. Set an interim milestone: In three weeks, select your first tentative job goals.

Does this conflict with my advice to know your company, to search for and understand its opportunities? Not at all. You should have developed this kind of background before. If you haven't, do the best you can in the six weeks. Having a reasonably good job goal will let you proceed with your planning. Sustaining your new mo-

mentum in career management is just as important as having a
good goal. It leads to a related subject: goal changes and stability.

CHANGING GOALS

Having a goal, any goal, and working toward it is more important
than what the goal is. I am not recommending that you change
your goal often or capriciously. I am recommending that when
you have a new idea, or when a new opportunity becomes available, consider it. Whether the new idea is a reasonable option
depends on where you are in your cycle and what commitments
you have at the time. If you are six months into a new job, your
commitments mean that you must forgo or postpone the new opportunity. If you're in your initial goal development, you're probably in an ideal situation to change. If you're eighteen months into
your present job, you probably can change if you haven't recently
made any additional commitments.

If you are launched on an educational goal, changing your job
goal may give you trouble. For example, if you're working on a
degree in accounting and an opportunity arises in Personnel, you
may lose some of the value of an accounting degree. A broader
educational program with limited specialization might be your
answer if you think you may change.

If your education or experience is in a specialized field, changing
to another field entails the risk that your knowledge of your original discipline will become obsolete. You probably can't avoid this,
but you can postpone it until you are certain of your new path.
Stay current by continuing to read, but also sustain your contacts
and discussions to have the assurance that you're keeping up.

You will not really test your job goal until you go through the
planning process to achieve it. But before you start planning, confirm that your new goal offers an opportunity for increased value

to yourself and your company. Even in its tentative stage, consider some of the possible growth opportunities that extend beyond it.

Don't fail to consider radical change opportunities. Some of them are the most fun.

Do you need to plan a possible escape route? The time to avoid being trapped is before you get into the situation—it's the one great opportunity of planning. It may be a part of your career planning that you keep to yourself.

SCHEDULING YOUR JOB GOAL

Set a basic schedule for your job goal. Don't hesitate; reach out and grab a date that seems slightly impossible. You will be tempted to creep up on it, to model each of your planned moves and set your goal date based on the sum of the estimated times.

That is not good! Real achievers plan by reaching out and grabbing the goal and then asking, "How can I make this happen?" Sure, they miss some schedules that way. They suffer a little, too, but their achievements are far superior. And they don't miss any more schedules than ol' Creepy Sureshot who sets the cushy goals—and their bosses know it.

Later, you may have to extend the date, but at least you will have tried. Although the goal you set impulsively may be too easy, most of the tough, interesting goals come from the arbitrary stretch approach.

PAY GOALS

Pay goals imply far more than simply money. Your pay, and the rate at which it is increasing, is a key factor always discussed by others when they are considering you for a new opportunity. Use pay goals in your planning, as a check on your progress toward the jobs that you select as goals. It's just as valuable to let your pay be a leading factor in developing your job goals. This is particularly important if you're planning vertical growth in your present field.

Fortunately, you only need a few basics to set meaningful pay goals. Approach the task two ways; you will get similar results.

1. If your company makes pay schedules available, locate your pay goal on that schedule. Even if the schedule changes, you can still chart your progress by looking at where the pay goal was originally.

2. The second approach is about as good and doesn't require a pay schedule. Assume that you are presently earning $2400 per month in job grade S2. This is about 9 percent above the minimum salary for your job grade. You are considering a tough goal— to achieve a similar position in job grade S6 in four years. On the present pay schedule this is a real-pay goal of about $3500 per month at that time. That is an average real-pay increase of about 10 percent for each of the four years. The dollars confirm what you already knew: Your selected work goal may be too tough, but it's on the edge of feasibility. If you want a tough challenge, take it.

Another way to develop challenging pay goals if you don't have a pay schedule is to cut through the confusing curtain of inflation and look at a few basics. The average person, at the peak real-pay of his or her career, earns a little less than twice the real-pay earned in the first year of work. The peak comes about twenty years into his or her career.

A little calculation indicates that Mr. Average earns an average annual real-pay raise of about 3 percent for each of those twenty years. In the early years, it's much higher; in the later years, it's much lower. Add about 6 percent for inflation (old rate), and the 3 percent becomes more like the 10 percent that most people think is an average raise in the early years.

Average people earn 6 to 7 percent real-pay increases in their first five years, and 1 to 2 percent increases in the last five years of their twenty years to reach peak earnings. Dedicated, effective people earn about twice the increases of average people in the early years. That's one thing that your plan is about—becoming one of those dedicated, effective people and earning twice the average real-pay raises. So, depending where you are in those first twenty years, take about 10 percent as a good goal and go with it. Now you are Mr. Dedicated, and you're back to the $3500 goal you selected the easy way.

Goal feasibilities change throughout your career. The previous examples can easily be valid for the first ten or fifteen years of your career. But if you stay average until age forty, you will acquire a low momentum that's hard to change. You can do it, but the preceding example is far too challenging for so late a start.

RESOURCE GOALS

The resources that you need to develop and grow in a particular job are different from those that you need to move yourself to a new, challenging opportunity. A repetitive cycle of these two processes is what makes up career development—get a new job, develop and contribute to job and self, get another new job, and so on.

You are your primary resource for your job change cycle. You can get some help from other people, but be aware that many of them will have positive aversions to helping with such things as deciding your goals. Your tactics are a real part of your resources for a job change. And your job knowledge is a personal resource over which you have significant control.

Job knowledge can be a diversionary trap that can stymie your whole career management. Consider two of its characteristics. First, learning is an innate satisfier. But don't let it become a soporific drug, a habit. Some people get hooked on education and don't recognize it as a habit. They avoid fulfilling their knowledge in meaningful work. If it does become a hobby, don't expect your company to award a prize for more unapplied learning and thus become frustrated when it doesn't.

Second, learning is a valuable activity that you can manage solely by yourself. You can go deep into an educational program without involving anyone in your company. This is a possible pitfall because you can get deeply committed and expended before you find that there's no market for your new learning in your company, or at least at working levels and pay that you need.

Develop your goals for education and training from needs that you identify when you plan your work. In a sense, the work goal is the market (demand side) and the knowledge is the supply side of the equation. I recognize that there is strong contrary opinion to this philosophy and accept that many successes have come from the reverse of my advice. In other words, some people get the education and then devise ways of using it. However, the contrary opinion fails to recognize the major satisfaction inherent in working with a good company of people, and the strong, innate needs for a continuing association with your company.

As you develop your goals for training and education, try to keep your supervisor involved. Even if your company has no formal educational assistance program, find out if it will pay for tuition and the costs of seminars.

Suppose it doesn't. If you regard the training as necessary, spend your own money. If you tried to sell it as having a good payoff for your company, it probably has a good enough payoff for you. It's regrettable if your company won't pay for it, but in most cases you're not talking about much more than a few car payments; you'll get most mileage out of the education. The same is true of subscriptions to trade and technical publications. If you will really get value from them, $20 to $100 is a modest personal cost compared with the probable return.

I will use contrasting examples to illustrate. First, assume that you're planning for vertical growth. You're Junior Buyer in Purchasing. Your goal is to manage commodity purchases in four years. You have easy decisions on resource goals in this case. Old standard: a degree in business administration is good. Courses in basic marketing or the basic technology of your company may be good. Seminars or short commercial courses in negotiating—original or refreshers—will be good. Getting support for this kind of directly usable information is easier.

Now take the tougher case, when you're planning a lateral move. Junior Buyer wants to convert to Junior Lawyer. This gives you an interesting tactical challenge. You may be able to sell your supervisor on supporting this on a company benefit basis and a frank appeal to support your career plan. More likely, you'll need to sweeten the pot with some up-front contributions to Purchasing.

In any case, this is a typical tactical challenge of the kind that you will face often. Start developing your capabilities to handle this kind of problem. Don't classify it as politics. Problems of this type are far simpler to resolve than the human relations problems that you handle in everyday living. The habit of planning gives you the time to anticipate this kind of problem and the time to solve it. When you think ahead, you don't have to be such a fast thinker. Job tactics are an essential resource for both your planning and execution. You will develop your latent capabilities, spurred by the game you're playing. Simply having a need and being aware of it will put you on the alert to the tactics of others. Adopt and modify tactics used by others to fit your own style.

As you plan, identify the help you need from other people. They become resources to you just as you are a resource to them. Develop techniques of how you use them as personal resources. Don't shrink from thinking that way.

Have no reservation about using them; you're in the company to work together toward shared goals. Use other people to execute your plans, and expect them to ask as freely for your help in achieving their goals. Limit your requests to immediate needs. Don't blabber and carry conversations from one to the other. Discuss your needs openly, but quietly. Limit your discussions of your goals and plans; you'll be glad when you make changes.

PLANNING

How do you plan your career? The answer depends on your goals and your cycle. In either of the two cases following, the tough part—setting your goals—is over for the moment. Planning is the fun part.

If your goal is to change the direction and pace of your career—make a lateral change—your basic problem is to plan how to get the new job, and what your initial contributions in the job will be.

If your present goal is vertical growth at a faster pace, you must plan how to get the next job up the ladder. But what is really different from the first case is that this problem centers first on how to improve your present job rather than on how to get another one. This means being innovative and changing the work that you're already doing, or making other changes to help improve your performance.

This same challenge occurs when you get an unsought assignment; your problem is really: "How do I make real improvements to today's work?" There was an opening; you were tapped; your goal was set for you. Create success in your new job. Even if it's tough, don't cry more than one day. Kick yourself and get to work.

In any of these cases, the basic pattern of planning is the same: Develop a model of the work in front of you, and get commitment from the people whose work you need and for the other necessary resources.

In recent years, model concepts for management have become familiar as powerful tools of achievement. Multiple techniques are available, but nearly all of them share similar fundamentals. You can use these same concepts as patterns for personal management. If you want extensive details of this kind of planning, read a manual on program evaluation review technique (PERT) or a comparable planning system. You don't have to apply it in every detail, but you can use its concepts of milestone achievements, schedules and schedule tradeoffs, and control techniques.

For your present need, start your planning model by defining a set of tasks (milestones) that will connect your present situation to your work goal. Assign a schedule to each of your tasks. Identify a resource. Decide who will perform each task.

If your starting goal is a simple one-notch step up in job grade, you can keep the simple model plan in your head. If your goals are grander, do your planning on paper. You can still keep it brief and simple. For example, if you're the single primary resource, omit that part of the model.

Take a look at how Junior Buyer stacks her goals:

Work Goal	Schedule (Months)
Junior buyer	Present
Buyer	12
Contract administrator	24
Legal administrator	48
Lawyer (pass bar exam)	60

Next, insert a few planning milestones in the first 24 months of the schedule:

Work Goal	Schedule	
Junior buyer	Present	
	3	Supervisor approval
	4	Start school
	6	New system for commodity buying
Buyer	12	
	18	Files, new system for commodity buying
		First contact contract administrator
Contract administrator	24	

This initial planning model is brief, but it may be all Junior Buyer needs. The alternative is to add several more milestones with completion dates. For example, she may indicate dates for preliminary discussions with her supervisor; she may want to discuss her long-range plan with a manager or an acquaintance in the Legal Department or a counselor in Personnel. (Generally, the more you picture on paper, the more you will understand what you have to do and what problems you will have, and the greater opportunity you will have to solve them.)

Note that buried in Junior Buyer's plan is the need for another, separate plan. Two milestones refer to a new system that she's planning in Purchasing, the sweetening of the pot for which we saw the need earlier. This is her innovation that will pave the way to Buyer. That plan will be quite different because any new system involves other people, and probably more diverse resources.

Junior Buyer has to be thinking about her tactics as she makes this plan. One of her first tactical decisions is when and how much to involve her supervisor. Should she—can she—discuss her goals and plan with the manager of the Legal Department? We can't tell whether she's developing her new purchasing system in the open, or as an "Underground Project." It is clear that she's depending on making system innovations to get early promotion to buyer.

This only scratches the surface of how you plan a career. It does touch on both main cycles. In the first years, the primary effort has to be on specific improvements in your present job. A much smaller and remote part, but just as important, is planning the new, growth jobs down the road.

INTERACTION: GOALS AND PLAN

You can't develop goals and plans as discreetly and independently as I have illustrated. While you generally want your goals to lead your planning, your plans may cause you to return to and modify your goals. If you reached for very tough goals, either tough tasks or tough schedules, you may be unable to develop a realistic plan to achieve them; you'll have to go back and rework your goals. This kind of looping is common to all good planning. But that's the way to do it; don't start with the easy, assured goals.

Don't hesitate to accept some possibility of slippage, or even failure, in your plans.

CONTROL

Control is the element of your system that keeps you on track. You're in control when you look ahead, anticipate the problems, and prevent their happening. I mentioned control earlier when I discussed scheduling; if you don't schedule a time to complete your job goals, they're open-ended and you can play with them forever. That's like an engineer who keeps polishing his design forever; he's never ready to manufacture.

Control, like the other elements of your personal system, involves the same concepts so well developed and commonly applied in business management systems. Many failures can be traced to failures to maintain the discipline of control.

You stay in control by using notes and a calendar. Put a big red X on your calendar on the same day of each month ahead. On that day, note the milestones you have completed.

On overdue milestones, set a new date. This is your test: If you continually miss your milestones, you will miss your goals. The primary purpose of milestones is interim control; you don't wait until the last minute to realize that you're going to miss your goal unless you make corrective action. My experience with people seeking job changes is that nearly all achieved their goals and schedules. Several succeeded so far ahead of schedule that they had a real challenge to catch up with the knowledge and skills that they needed.

It was this kind of experience in my first major use of personal control that stunned me with the power of the system. I took what

I thought was a tough schedule goal for a radical change. What I planned for three years took only two.

As I have said, several who failed to get the job they sought have been surprised to be offered different, equally good, jobs soon after.

GETTING HELP

On this, I offer both bad news and good news. The bad news for job changes is that you can expect to do most of your career management yourself. Don't expect much help in your actual management process.

The good news is that you won't need much help, for several reasons: First, everyone I know or work with who has made a commitment to take charge and change his or her career has been able to do it; even people in ten- or twenty-year ruts (their word) break free and begin to manage themselves. Second, if you manage yourself, you will be offered more good help than you can use in executing your plan.

Stay aware of the things you must do yourself. *You* must define your goals, decide what work will satisfy you, and the rewards that you need from that work. *You* must make your plans and commit the momentum for their accomplishment. If you are lucky, you may find someone to talk to, to test your plans and tactics on, someone who will be your devil's advocate. Your chance for this is 10 percent.

Be careful in placing reliance on two customary sources for help—your supervisors and school counselors. They may be able to help you, but be sure you understand their perspectives, their biases.

Most supervisors don't know any more about career management than you do. When this is the case, you're lucky if they don't try to help you. Finding out is easy. But before you do, confirm that your career intentions will not upset your primary work relationship with your supervisor. Consider whether he or she will regard you as a competitor or prefer that you continue to do your present work. These and other problems can be solved, but anticipate their possibility.

If your supervisor demonstrates clear understanding of your goals and plans and encourages you, ask for assistance. He or she has a unique opportunity to help you. Your supervisor's counsel and understanding will be important, but his or her motivation and expectation for you will be more so.

Reserve the same kind of judgment for school counseling. Good school counselors are a good source of help and advice for achieving an educational goal. Even if they have extensive experience working in business and industry, be careful of their viewpoints. Don't substitute their perspectives of work, business, company, and careers for your own. Consider for yourself whether they are overly biased by their work field and whether academic attitudes have distorted their viewpoint of the business work environment.

THE CONTRARY VIEW

Many of the attitudes I have urged you to adopt are challenged by others. For instance, I have urged you to look for your career goals in your company and its work. This is the opposite of the advice of most authorities and people who dominate counseling. They tell you to look inside yourself first when you look for career goals. But I say that work is fundamentally satisfying, that work is doing what has value to someone else—your company. Look outside of yourself; join with others in your company in reaching for challenging goals. There lies your primary hope for satisfaction in your career.

The other example of where I differ is in the importance I suggest you place on goals for pay. This mask we put over the importance of pay seems to be some combination of puritan ethic and management plot. Regardless of our intents and our systems, assignments of pay rates are arbitrary. This makes for many uncomfortable conversations. We collude because many of us are reluctant to admit the importance we assign to pay.

I offer these people this analogy: Your company's purpose is to serve its customers needs, but your company's incentive for this work is the profit it earns. Earning the pay you need is comparable to your company's need for profit as a respectable personal incentive. It shows that you are getting your share of your company's success.

Index